Anthropological Papers
Museum of Anthropology, University of Michigan
No. 76

Primitive Polluters
Semang Impact on the
Malaysian Tropical Rain Forest Ecosystem

by
A. Terry Rambo

Ann Arbor, Michigan
1985

© 1985 The Regents of The University of Michigan
The Museum of Anthropology
All rights reserved

Printed in the
United States of America
ISBN 0-915703-04-1

To Elman R. Service

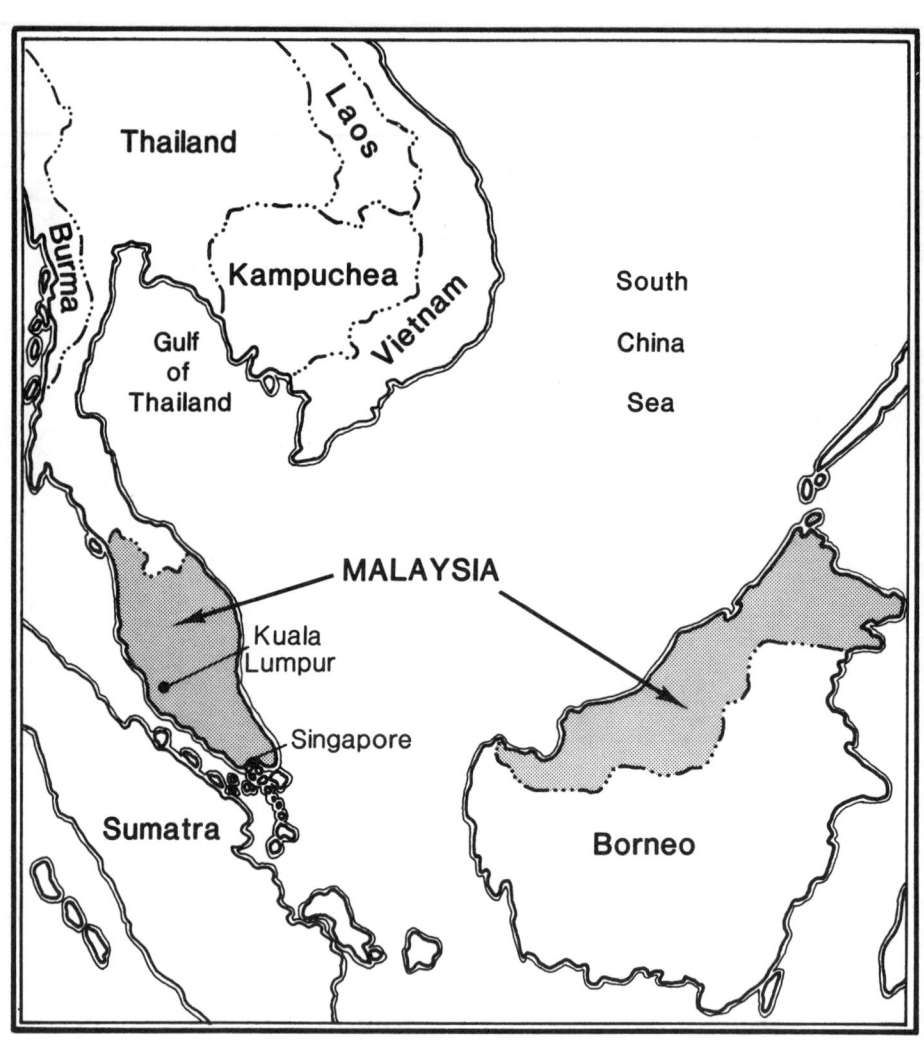

Contents

Figures	vi
Tables	vi
Plates	vii
Foreword	ix
Preface	xv
1. Introduction	1
2. A Conceptual Framework for Studying Human Impacts on the Environment	9
3. The Semang and Their Ecosystem	29
4. The Impact of the Semang on Their Ecosystem	47
5. Conclusions: The Evolution of Human Relations with the Environment	77
Plates	81
References	99

Figures

1. Location of the Semang resettlement at Sungai Rual — 5
2. The systems model of human ecology — 11
3. The Semang in relation to their ecosystem — 39
4. Comparison of air temperature and relative humidity in settlement and undisturbed forest — 55
5. Comparison of soil and water temperatures in settlement and undisturbed forest — 56

Tables

1. Suspended sediment levels in river water — 60
2. Dissolved solids levels in river water — 60
3. Organic component as percentage of dissolved solids in river water — 61
4. Soil loss due to rainfall impact — 66
5. Birds observed in settlement area at Sungai Rual — 74

Plates

1. A Semang band returns to the settlement from a collecting trip in the forest — 83
2. Traditional-style lean-tos — 84
3. A Semang family inside their lean-to — 85
4. The resettlement at Sungai Rual — 86
5. Malay-style house in the resettlement area — 87
6. Living area underneath a house in the resettlement area — 88
7. Semang man clearing rubbish away from his front door — 89
8. Semang man heating blowpipe darts — 90
9. Felling a tree in the primary forest to clear a swidden — 91
10. Semang woman clearing undergrowth to make a new swidden — 92
11. Semang woman carrying home firewood from the forest — 93
12. Semang hunters bringing wild pig meat home from the forest — 94
13. Semang women shelling *petai* seeds — 95
14. Semang boy holding captive wild birds — 96
15. Smoke drifting through he roof of a house in the resettlement — 97
16. A young Semang male drinking tea in a shop in Kampung Jeli — 98

Foreword

by
Jeffrey R. Parsons
Museum of Anthropology, University of Michigan

A quarter century ago Terry Rambo and I were students of Elman R. Service at the University of Michigan. That was an especially exciting time to be studying anthropology in Ann Arbor, for in those years were gathered here an exceptional group of scholars who were asking important questions about cultural evolution and coming up with innovative and exciting answers. One of the reasons it was exciting for students was because many of these questions crosscut subdisciplinary and interdisciplinary boundaries. I recall that Service's courses appealed equally strongly to archaeologists like myself, to ethnologists like Terry Rambo, and to a range of other social science interests as well. Service's courses and ideas appealed so broadly because they could often illuminate or structure specific research interests so diverse as, for example, the development of prehistoric civilizations, the organization of tribal exchange, the structure of chiefly polity, or the relationships between cultural behavior and gene frequency change over time.

It was at about that time that Elman Service's path-breaking book, *Primitive Social Organization: An Evolutionary Perspective,* appeared. I well recall how exciting it was to read in it about bands, tribes, chiefdoms and states, and then to hear the author in lectures or seminars further develop his reasoning about particular points that he felt were especially important (such as tribal sodalities or chiefly redistribution or the role of patrilineal kinship in "pristine" bands). I recall how I would go back and forth, between book and classroom, thinking about Service's models, about how they had been developed, and about how they might become useful in the archaeological research I was getting involved in. I think it was in this context that I first began to reflect seriously on how an anthropologist designs research, collects data, and analyzes and interprets these data. It is obvious that Terry Rambo and many other students who encountered Elman Service and other anthropologists at Michigan during that era were also going through comparable intellectual experiences.

It has been widely recognized for a long time that Elman Service's ideas expressed in such works as *Primitive Social Organization* have had an enormous impact across anthropology, and perhaps especially in the subfield of archaeology. Perhaps somewhat less well known is the penetrating, critical approach to the ethnographic data base that Service used to develop his own ideas. I would like to dwell briefly on this dimension of Elman Service as a scholar and teacher, particularly since it relates so directly to some aspects of *Primitive Polluters*. One of Service's special concerns in the classroom was to impart a notion of how important it was to critically evaluate the ethnographic record as a source of insight into prehistoric social organization. He took special pains to make students realize that ethnographers had sometimes been misled by appearances. One of his favorite examples, at least the one that has stuck best in my own memory, was the tendency of some ethnographers to associate "primitive" forms of social organization (by which he meant small, egalitarian, generalized, and kin-based) with living people who didn't wear pants or Mother Hubbards; i.e., a notion that if people looked "primitive" because they didn't wear modern clothes and didn't use many of the other material trappings of modern society, then their social organization was also likely to be "primitive." Having said this, he would then proceed to drive home the point that sometimes people who had long been in direct or indirect contact with European society and whose social organization had been profoundly affected by adapting to Europeans didn't wear pants because they were simply too poor to buy them, or were otherwise unable or unwilling to adopt Western dress. I recall that he referred specifically in this regard to such groups as early twentieth century inhabitants of the Paraguayan Gran Chaco, whom he regarded as essentially refugees produced by several centuries of harassment by more powerful neighbors who had ultimately pushed the Chacoan groups into a marginal region that nobody else cared much about. His main point, of course, was that a group of people can superficially look quite "primitive" but not necessarily represent a pristine form of societal organization "left over" from an earlier era due to isolation from the larger world.

This same general theme is an important part of Terry Rambo's main message in *Primitive Polluters,* though the specific emphasis is somewhat different. Rambo is here more concerned with cultural universals than he is with the organizational implications of Semang contacts with the larger world, and their involvement as "professional" hunters and gatherers within a much larger economic system which supplies some of their most basic needs. Nevertheless, we see in *Primitive Polluters* an expression of some of the same concerns that Elman Service had about penetrating superficial appearances to discover counter-intuitive dimensions of human cultural behavior. To understand Semang impact on the tropical forest ecosystem, it is necessary, as Rambo emphasizes so strongly, to understand their close economic relationship to the external world. This relationship introduces into the Semang ecosystem things like rice, shotgun shells, cigarettes, metal tools, transistor radios, and flashlight batteries, while it removes such items as *kerdas* seeds, *Ubi* and *Jogoh* roots, monkeys, bamboo, and human labor. Archaeological evidence, as scattered and incomplete as it still is, suggests a long time depth throughout Southeast Asia for this kind of exchange between forest products, on the one hand, and certain food staples and craft goods, on the other. The suggestion is that many (perhaps most) Southeast Asian hunters and gatherers have for centuries and even millennia been a specialized component of much larger complex cultural systems. For an anthropologist interested in cultural evolution, the really fascinating and provocative hypothesis is that the specific "primitive" qualities of people like the Semang represent an adaptation to external demands for the forest products which they (the Semang, etc.) control access to.

Primitive Polluters contributes to the ongoing and multi-faceted development of this important hypothesis by providing a finely textured ecosystem analysis at the most basic level in the long chain which links a small Semang band to the modern nation states. With his measurements of precipitation, sediment loads, soil temperatures, and air quality, Rambo is pursuing some of the same basic questions about cultural adaptation and change raised years ago by Elman Service in his classes at the University of Michigan and in his writings. Perhaps Rambo's study departs most notably from Service's orientation in that it emphasizes basic similarities, rather than basic differences, between "primitive" and "civilized" cultures. By emphasizing similarities, Rambo helps provide new insights into some old questions. By implication he forces us to consider the extent to which existing evolutionary typologies (which, at least in archaeology, are still largely those of Elman Service) may not do full justice to the degree to which large complex organizations (i.e., states) have modified, or even created, some of the cultural forms we now regard as developmentally antecedent in the general trajectory of cultural evolution. A decade ago Morton Fried* raised this very issue, but it seems to have received less attention in recent years than it deserves.

Cultural evolution is probably a less central issue in contemporary ethnology than it was some 20 years ago. On the other hand, in anthropological archaeology interest in evolution has increased dramatically over the same period. For whatever reasons this shift has occurred, it appears that Service's ideas about cultural evolution, presented so cogently and succinctly in the early 1960s, reached North American archaeologists just as they were making their first really systematic efforts to use the archaeological record to study evolutionary processes, and when they badly needed a theoretical framework within which to structure their research. This may be why archaeologists have found Service's work so useful and stimulating, and why they continue so energetically in their attempts to refine or modify his models. Here too may be found some additional insight into Service's own long-time interest in prehistory and archaeological research (e.g., Service 1941).†

I recall that very soon after we first met in 1961, Elman Service asked me about recent work in Mesoamerican archaeology that related to the complex interrelationships between land use, environment, and social organization for prehistoric groups in the Lowland Maya area and in central Mexico. He often considered these kinds of ecological questions in class, and it was always clear to me that he found an ecological perspective attractive. Thus, it comes as no surprise to see that Terry Rambo, my fellow student from that era, attributes to Service some of the basic conceptual foundation that underlies his own anthropological orientation. I think that as Elman Service reads *Primitive Polluters* he will have occasion to consider its implications for some of the problems we used to talk about in the early 1960s: for example, the collapse of Classic Maya states in the lowland tropical forests of southern Mesoamerica, and the deterioration of large-scale hydraulic agricultural systems in the arid plains of Mesopotamia and Coastal Peru. We now know a lot more about these kinds of problems than we did two and a half decades ago, but we are still searching for clear, definitive answers about cause and effect relationships.

I think *Primitive Polluters* is going to be a very important datum in the

---

* Fried, Morton H. *The Notion of the Tribe.* 1975. Menlo Park, Calif.: Cummings Publishing Co.

† Service, E.R. *Lithic Patina as an Age Criterion.* Papers of the Michigan Academy of Science, Arts and Letters, 27.

larger task of getting better answers to these questions about cause and effect because it suggests so clearly some of the places where anthropologists ought to be looking for more and better information. Furthermore, it suggests that the well-known prehistoric ecological crises to which I have referred above are likely to have had their roots in more subtle changes that occurred slowly in localized settings, but whose impact steadily accumulated and expanded in the course of growing complexity. *Primitive Polluters,* of course, provides no really definitive answers to these larger issues. However, it forcefully reminds us that some big problems may be qualitatively little different from some small problems, and it provides us with the beginnings of a conceptual strategy for dealing innovatively with the kinds of big problems and big questions that Elman Service has outlined so forcefully over the course of three decades.

Preface

In 1958 I enrolled in the University of Michigan as a freshman in journalism. Compelled to take a course in social science by the University's then sacrosanct distribution requirements, I opted for Introductory Anthropology, taught by Professor Elman R. Service. This chance decision, made in the frenzy of registration in Waterman Gymnasium, would lead ultimately to my doing the research among the Semang in the Malaysian rain forest on which this monograph is based. I found Service's approach to understanding the human condition fascinating; in the spring semester I not only signed up for a second course with him, but changed my major to anthropology as well.

In subsequent years others would strongly influence my approach to the discipline, particularly Mischa Titiev and Eric R. Wolf at the University of Michigan, and Alice G. Dewey and Henry T. Lewis at the University of Hawaii, but it was Service from whom I first heard the the sorts of questions about cultural systems and their evolution that I am still trying to answer. Given this background, I was immensely pleased when the University of Michigan Museum of Anthropology accepted this monograph for its Anthropological Papers series. Publishing it in this way allows me to repay, at least in small part, an outstanding intellectual debt to the institution where my professional enculturation as an anthropologist began.

In doing this research a number of additional professional debts have been incurred. Field work was supported by a University of Malaya staff research grant. Professor Yip Yat-Hoong, then Deputy Vice Chancellor for Research, was unfailing in his support as was Professor Kahar Bador, head of the Department of Anthropology and Sociology where I was a lecturer. Drs. Colin Leigh and Low Kwai Sim of the University of Malaya Department of Geography and Professor Jose Furtado of the Department of Zoology provided much helpful advice on measuring various environmental impacts and generously loaned me needed instruments and supplies.

This research could not have been carried out without the assistance of the Malaysian Government's Department of Orang Asli Affairs (JOA). Dr. Baharon Azhar bin Raffie'i, Director General of the department, and his staff were always helpful in making necessary field arrangements. Special thanks are due Encik Abdullah Hassan, the JOA field officer responsible for the Semang settlement at Sungai Rual, for his hospitality and the generosity with which he shared his knowledge of the area.

Assistance in collecting data in the field was provided by several of my students at the University of Malaya including Abdul Rashid Idris, Alias Mohd. Ali, Koh Bee Hong, and, particularly, Alberto G. Gomes. Successive drafts of this manuscript were typed by Katijah Binte Abdul Karim and Lyn Mukai. Kate Gillogly assisted in compiling the bibliography and made many helpful editorial suggestions. Sally Horvath of the University of Michigan Museum of Anthropology was responsible for final editing and layout of this volume. Karl Hutterer, Neil Jamieson, George Lovelace and Dawn Rambo all read various earlier drafts and made useful suggestions for improvements in the text.

1
Introduction

That all human societies, primitive as well as civilized, cause environmental change, often the sort of degradation popularly referred to as "pollution," is the major premise of this monograph. It is further argued that such change is the inevitable consequence of the functioning of human social systems rather than a reflection of any particular cultural values regarding human interactions with nature. People change the environment, not because they necessarily desire to do so, but because as participants in social systems they have no choice in the matter. In order to function as the superorganisms they are, social systems must take energy and materials from natural ecosystems and inject their wastes back into these systems. It is these interactions that cause environmental change and since all social systems, regardless of evolutionary complexity, engage in such exchanges, all must inevitably produce some environmental impact.

The view of human relations with the environment expressed above is contrary to much that has been said on the subject. In fact, it is fair to say that the opposite view—that primitive peoples live in harmony with nature whereas civilized societies wantonly degrade their environments—has achieved the status of conventional wisdom. Certainly it was an unquestioned assumption of many leaders of the environmental movement of the late 1960s and early 1970s that degradation of the natural environment was a sin unique to modern Western industrial society. Environmental activists repeatedly contrasted the greedy exploitation of natural resources by modern Americans with the supposedly loving care given nature by American Indians and other indigenous peoples. Charles Reich, whose book *The Greening of America* served as a manifesto for the countercultural movement, wrote:

> In all societies prior to the modern, no matter how diverse in other ways, there existed an essential harmony between the people and the land, a harmony in which nature was not violently altered or violated. Modern society makes war on nature. A competitive market uses nature as a commodity to be exploited—turned into profit. [1970:28]

The historian Lynn White gave scholarly respectability to this dogma with his widely cited article "The Historical Roots of Our Ecologic Crisis" (1967), in which he attributed Western destruction of the environment to adherence to the Judeo-Christian ethic of human dominance over nature. Marxist-oriented writers for their part saw ecological degradation as the inevitable concommitant of capitalism in which the exploitation of humans by each other was mirrored by their equally ruthless exploitation of nature.

According to the prevailing view, the character of human relations with the environment was determined by cultural values. Stopping the destruction of nature by Western societies demanded, therefore, an ethical reformation, a return to the environmental ethos said to characterize precapitalist cultures.

The view that Western values are uniquely responsible for environmental destruction has been challenged, notably by Tuan Yi-fu (1968). Tuan pointed out that classical Chinese society had also caused massive environmental degradation despite its adherence to Confucian values stressing harmony between people and nature. As the Chinese example reveals, the activities of any large-scale human society, regardless of its cultural values towards nature, must inevitably have disruptive impact on natural ecosystems. Human relations with nature, therefore, are not determined by ideology alone. Instead, they reflect the operation of the whole cultural system, including the interaction between population, technology, social structure, and values.

The extent to which the small-scale societies using traditional technology—those societies that anthropologists have usually labeled as "primitive"—alter the natural environment has remained an open question, however. Eric Wolf (1982:91) asserts that food-collecting bands "do not transform nature, but gather up and concentrate for human use resources naturally available in the environment." Following Marx's lead, he claims that "the natural environment is not a means for humanly controlled organic transformations, as is cultivation or herding; it is 'the object of labor' but not its 'instrument.'"

John Bodley (1976) claims that traditional peoples almost always live in essential harmony with their environment. Primitive cultures are seen as representing the only truly successful long-term ecological adaptation. Modern industrial societies, on the other hand, have fallen into an evolutionary trap and are fated for early extinction once they exhaust the nonrenewable resources on which they depend, or poison themselves with the pollutants which they emit into the environment in ever growing quantities.

Others have admitted that even the most technologically primitive societies produced at least some environmental degradation. Its ecological significance is discounted, however, as being no more than a faint foreshadowing of the dramatic changes to be wrought by industrial societies. Nicholson (1971:12) writes, for example, that

> while numbers remained small and localized early pressures through food gathering and primitive hunting and fishing can have made no appreciable impact on the environment. The emergence of added demands for clothing, shelter and tools appears significant only as the first clear indicator of the eventually insatiable demands which man was destined to make upon natural resources.

In a like vein, Philip E.L. Smith (1972:12) comments that

> during the several million years of the Pleistocene, the numerous foraging groups around the world probably had very little direct impact on their physical environments. Man's forest and grass fires may have created temporary changes, he may have aided in the extinction of some of the animals he hunted..., and the immediate environs of his larger encampments or villages may have suffered some degradation. But with the development of larger communities after food production and with the expansion of both population and subsistence, the human potentiality for environmental modification and resource depletion was greatly increased.

An intermediate position has been taken by Bennett (1976:244) who argues that while most of our environmental "... destructive potential has emerged late in human history... the behavioral capacities responsible for this pattern were present in Homo sapiens from the beginning," a view also held by Guthrie (1971).

Only a few scholars have taken the position that all human societies, whether primitive or advanced, have produced significant environmental impacts. This view was clearly articulated by Heizer (1955:1) who argued that

> ... at any point in time or space man has occupied a region he has materially affected the soil, the fauna, the flora, and even the climate, through the intermediacy of that one distinctive possession which we call culture.

Harp (1974:15) holds a similar position:

> recently it has become fashionable to condemn ourselves as despoilers of the natural environment.... However, we err in thinking of this as a phenomenon only of the past several decades, or even of the Industrial Age, for man has been a major factor in the evolution of the earth's surface for perhaps the last two million years, or at least since he acquired control of fire in the middle of the Pleistocene period.... Pursuant to his proliferation of culture and his deployment of it as a shield and a set of techniques to mediate between himself and nature, he effected profound changes in preexisting natural ecological processes.

As is so often the case in ideologically-charged controversies, little attempt has been made to empirically test the opposed points of view. Anthropological field workers have, on the whole, paid little attention to the environmental impacts of the societies they have studied, leading Bennett (1976:266) to observe that

> ... the case probably can never be proven because the ethnological literature so often lacks critical information on social aspects of environmental exploitation, resource magnitudes, and the effects of environmental use over long periods of time.

I.G. Simmons (1974:56) also points out the inadequacy of available ethnographic evidence on the impact of primitive peoples on their ecosystems:

> the evidence from modern hunters is so scanty and of such an indifferent kind for our purposes that it is scarcely possible to come to a firm conclusion about whether lands occupied by them are virgin lands, i.e., have unmanipulated ecosystems.

A Field Study of Semang Impacts On the Environment

In the face of this lack of empirical data on the environmental impact of primitive cultures, I decided to carry out a field study specifically aimed at assessing the impact on the tropical rain forest ecosystem of the Semang Orang Asli of Peninsular Malaysia. The Semang, or Negritos as they are often labeled, are described in many ethnology texts as one of the most primitive surviving human societies. Living in small bands that obtain their living by hunting, fishing, foraging, and sporadic shifting cultivation, the Semang would appear to be an almost perfect instrument for measuring environmental change caused by primitive societies.

Ideally, this study should have been conducted with one of the few remaining fully nomadic Semang bands. Unfortunately, security conditions in 1976 precluded carrying out such field work and it was necessary instead to study a group of Jahai-speaking Semang who had been regrouped three years earlier into what was intended to be a permanent settlement by the Department of Aboriginal Affairs (JOA). The group selected for study was located at Rual Post, approximately ten kilometers west of Jeli, in Tanah Merah District just south of the Kelantan border with Thailand (Fig. 1).

At Rual Post, six bands having a total population of 184 persons had been brought together into a single settlement in 1972. A school and clinic were established by the JOA to provide a focal point for the settlement. The Semang were encouraged by provision of food rations to clear forest land and plant subsistence crops and rubber and fruit trees. It was the

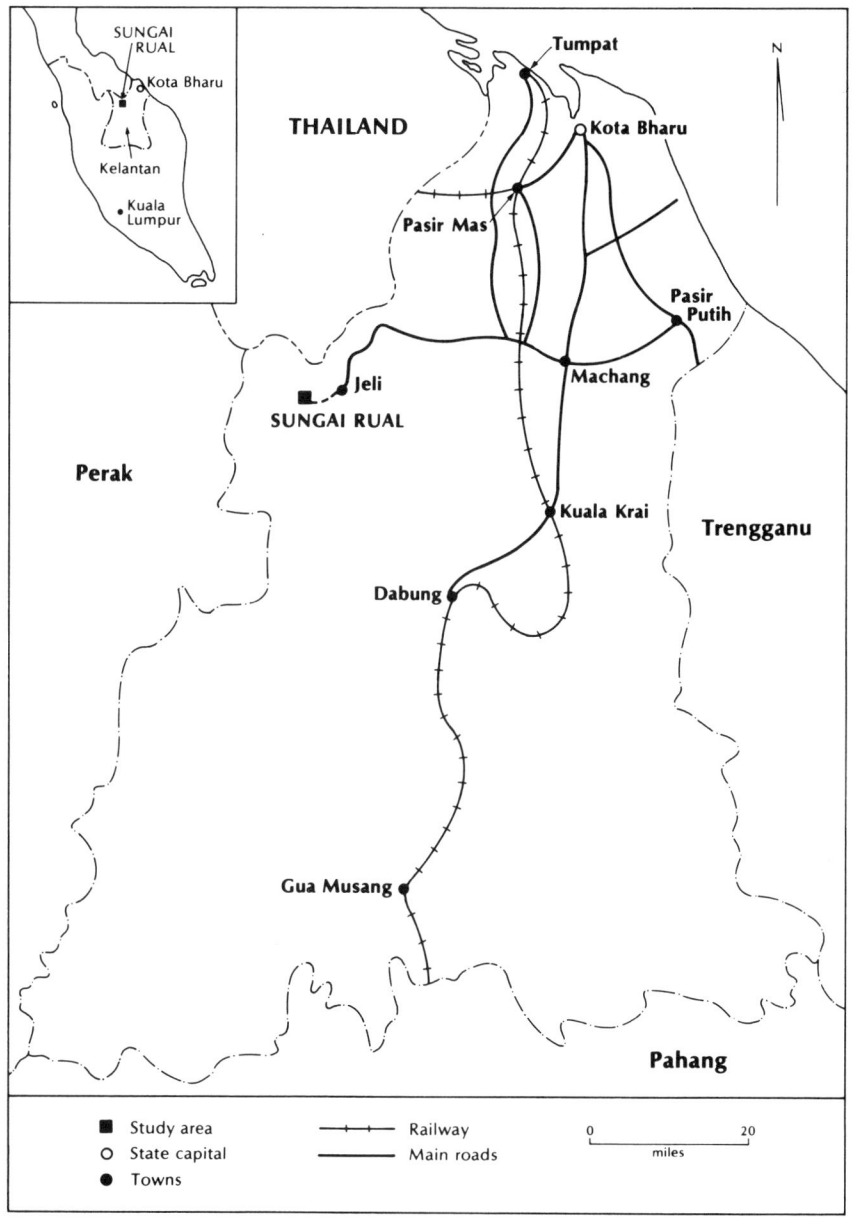

Figure 1. Location of the Semang resettlement at Sungai Rual. Reprinted, by permission, from Gomes, 1982, Fig. 1.

government's hope to convert the Semang into sedentary farmers living in a Malay style village. Members of some of the bands did construct semipermanent houses on stilts in the Malay style. Others, however, continued to live in Semang style lean-tos, shifting their campsites every few days in the forest surrounding the resettlement area. Even the groups residing in permanent houses stayed at the settlement only when government rations were available, resuming their nomadic wandering in the forest whenever supplies ran out. Rual Post had become a fixed point around which they moved and all groups returned to the settlement frequently, especially during the school term when every child attending classes received a generous food ration which was shared with the entire family.

Although resettlement has caused some changes in the people's life style, they continue to a large extent to follow traditional Semang customs and to interact with the forest environment much as they have for hundreds of years. The greater population density and lowered mobility of the resettlement population have tended to intensify the impact of the Semang on their ecosystem but these differences are matters of degree rather than kind.

Field work was carried out among the Semang at Rual Post on three occasions: a preliminary exploratory visit for five days (August 20 through 24, 1975), a one month stay (April 10 through May 10, 1976) during which most of the data presented in this report were collected, and a nine day visit (April 9 through 17, 1978) to fill in gaps in the original study and observe the consequences of resettlement over time.

On each visit I was accompanied by several of my students from the Department of Anthropology and Sociology of the University of Malaya. Three of these students (Alias Mohd. Ali, Abdul Rashid Idris, and Alberto Gomes) have written graduation exercises reporting the results of their own studies. Alberto Gomes has also included data collected on these trips and a subsequent visit in 1979 into his Master's thesis (Gomes 1979) and a research report published by the East-West Environment and Policy Institute (Gomes 1982).

Field research was carried out employing standard ethnographic methods, particularly observation and interviewing of key informants. Lack of proficiency in either Jahai or Bahasa Malaysia, the lingua franca employed by the Semang in their dealings with outsiders, forced me to rely more on observation than would usually be the case in a more extended field study. I also made frequent use of my Malay-speaking students as interpreters. Methods used to collect ecological data are described in chapter 4.

The findings of this research project are presented in the following chapters. Chapter 2 discusses the conceptual approach employed in this study; chapter 3 describes the Semang social system in relation to the ecosystem; chapter 4 presents findings on Semang impact on their environment; and chapter 5 sets forth conclusions derived from this research.

2
A Conceptual Framework for Studying Human Impacts on the Environment

The present study falls within the domain of human ecology—the study of human interactions with the environment. The specific conceptual framework employed is that of the systems model of human ecology (Rambo 1982a; 1983). Although employed to understand relations between human behavior and the natural environment, the systems model is a culturological one. It focuses on how humans, organized into social systems by shared cultural beliefs and values, interact with nature. In its focus on the social system as the key adaptive unit, it differs from most other approaches to human ecology. These have generally focused on the survival of humans as biological organisms, treating them as ecologically identical to other animal species.

The so-called "general ecology" advocated by Andrew Vayda and Roy Rappaport (1968) identified the "local population" as the appropriate unit of analysis in human ecology. Culture was of interest only as it could be shown to contribute to the survival of this biologically defined population. More recently, the "actor-based model" of human ecology (Orlove 1980), which is concerned with how individual human beings make decisions contributing to their survival, has enjoyed considerable popularity. On the whole, users of this model have ignored culture as an aspect of human adaptation, treating individuals as totally rational decision-makers who always make ecologically optimum choices ensuring the individual the highest probability of survival.

In contrast, the systems model of human ecology is principally concerned with the evolution and persistence over time of what Leslie White (1975) referred to as "cultural systems" and what I call here "social systems." Recognizing the dialectical relationship between culture and nature as a major driving force in evolutionary change, the model focuses attention on interactions between the human social system and the ecosystem. Each system retains its integrity as a separate system, with each changing its structural configuration according to its own internal dynamics. At the same time, however, it is recognized that each system receives inputs of energy, materials, and information from the other, and that these inputs also influence its structure and functioning. Each system, of course, is also open to influence from other systems of the same kind so that a social system may be altered by inputs received from a neighboring social system (the processes called diffusion and acculturation by anthropologists) just as an ecosystem may be changed by inputs from other ecosystems (e.g., migration and colonization, inflows of pollutants or sediments). Causality in the systems model of human ecology is thus extremely complex with no *a priori* assignment of prime mover status to any element or force in the total system. Figure 2 is a simplified diagram of the basic relationships involved in the systems model of human ecology.

The systems model emphasizes four relational aspects:

1) Inputs from the ecosystem into the social system. These inputs can be in the form of energy (e.g., food, petroleum), materials (e.g., protein, construction materials), or information (e.g., sounds, visual stimuli).

2) Inputs from the social system into the ecosystem. Again, these can take the form of energy, materials, or information generated by human activities.

3) Changes in the institutions making up the social system in response to inputs from the ecosystem. Such changes may either be primary, as when an increase in the death rate due to environmentally transmitted diseases changes the population structure of a society, or secondary, as when other social system institutions change in response to environmentally generated primary change in one institution. Social systems' changes in response to inputs from the ecosystem may be, and often are, adaptive, i.e., they contribute to the continuing survival of the social system under changed environmental conditions. They need not, however, result in a better or happier way of life for individual human participants. In other words, the social system itself, rather than the people who are involved in it, is the unit of natural selection and adaptation.

4) Changes in the ecosystem in response to inputs from the social system. Just as human society changes in response to environmental influences, so does the ecosystem change in response to human influences. Such change

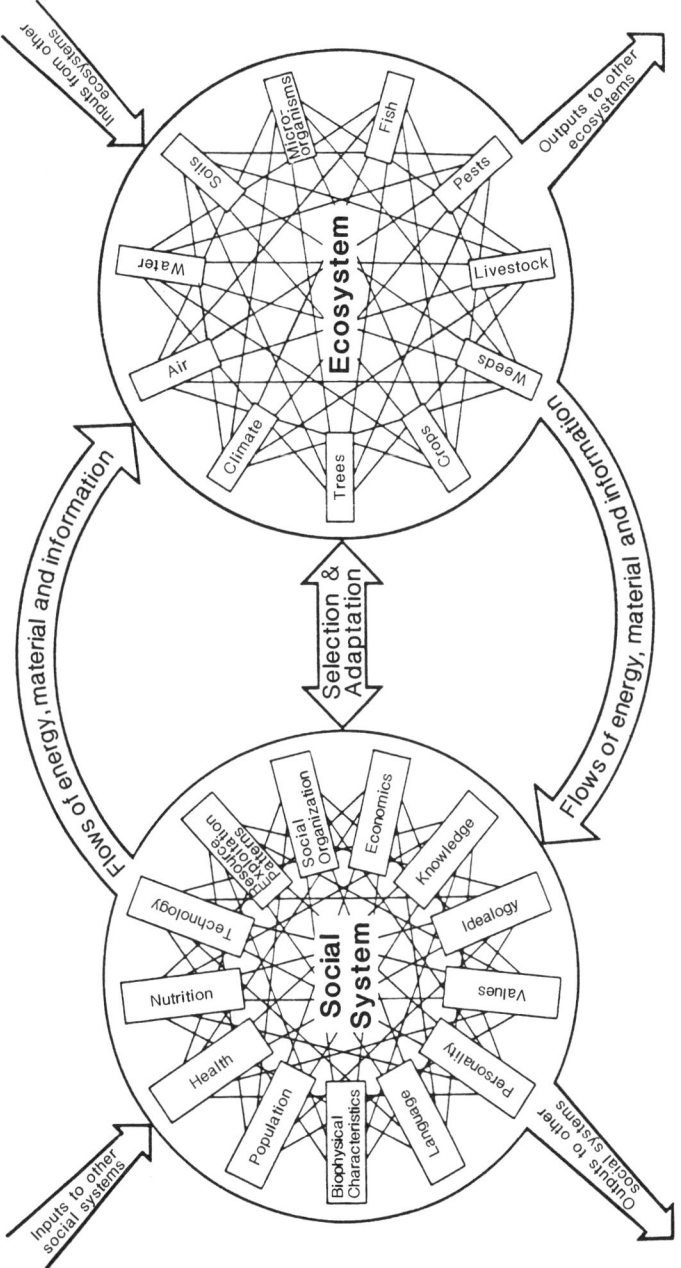

Figure 2. The systems model of human ecology. Adapted from Rambo, 1982, Fig. 2.

may be either primary, the direct impact of a human activity on an ecosystem component, e.g., the killing off of a particular animal species by overhunting; or secondary, alterations in other ecosystem components caused by anthropogenic primary change in one component.

The present study is focused only on the last mentioned concern of human ecology; the description of changes occurring in the ecosystem in response to inputs from the social system. These human impacts on the ecosystem can, for analytic purposes, be divided into four basic categories: deposition, destruction, disruption, and dissemination. Each of these four types of impact is described in turn below using illustrations drawn primarily from tropical Asia and the Pacific.

Deposition

Deposition is often called "pollution." Although in popular usage pollution refers to any environmental disturbance resulting from human activities (it is employed in this sense in the title of this book), in scientific usage pollution means the introduction into an ecosystem of energy, materials, or information in quantities sufficient to disrupt the normal functioning of the system. Technically speaking, therefore, pollution is always a relative condition, determined by the difference in magnitude between the quantity of inputs and the size of the affected system. There is always exchange of energy, materials, and information between the human social system and its ecosystem, but only when the quantities involved become too large for the existing channels within the systems to handle is it appropriate to speak of pollution. Thus, for the twenty members of a Semang band to use a large jungle river as their toilet does not necessarily constitute pollution; in fact productivity of fish may actually be increased by such enrichment of the nutrient-poor tropical river waters. If a city of 200,000 persons should dump its untreated sewage into the same river, however, the result is water pollution in an extreme form. The additional energy and materials deposited into the river, far from increasing fish production, will totally destroy it since the demand for oxygen by the microorganisms engaged in decomposing the sewage will completely consume all dissolved oxygen in the river. On the other hand, that same quantity of urban sewage, if properly composted and spread over a sufficient area of farm land, as is done in China, would be a valuable manure rather than a pollutant, serving to enhance ecosystem productivity in ways beneficial to the human population. Of course, information on the presence in the ecosystem of the manure, transmitted to the noses of the human population in the form of strong odors, might also be considered to be a form of pollution by some of its recipients.

In the case of such information flow, definition of what constitutes pollution becomes particularly difficult. To the astronomer, the light reflected into the night sky from urban areas which obscures the view of the stars through a telescope undoubtedly constitutes pollution; to city dwellers, fearful of robbers and muggers, the brighter the lights, the more secure they feel. Similarly, while the nature lover may enjoy walking deep inside a forest with no sign of human presence, the average person, especially of urban origin, is made vaguely uncomfortable or even frightened by the absence of any sign that one's own kind are near. I well remember the unexpected sense of pleasure I felt when, after walking alone for two days across an uninhabited rain forest in Central America, I came across a small pile of rusting tin cans marking the abandoned campsite of some earlier exploring party. To have found the same old tins in a park or nature reserve would have thrown me into a rage against the thoughtless "litter bug" who had so carelessly despoiled the scenic landscape, but in the deep jungle they only made me feel somehow less lonely. The point is not, of course, that it is a good thing to litter in jungles and a bad thing in parks, but that what constitutes informational pollution is highly subject to cultural interpretation.

Given the fact that excessive deposition of just about anything can constitute pollution, it is rather pointless to present any sort of comprehensive list of possible pollutants. More useful, perhaps, will be to examine some of the effects that pollution can have on the principal components of the ecosystem—the air, soil, water, and plants and animals.

Air Pollution

It is usual to think of two major types of air pollution, caused respectively by particulate matter and gases. Heat, sound, and light are also transmitted through the air, though, and can be significant forms of pollution as well.

Particulate matter can be present in the atmosphere either in the form of solids, e.g., dust, pollen grains or ash, or as liquids, in the form of aerosols and chemicals dissolved in water droplets. It is particulates in the form of smoke, soot, and dust that urban dwellers are most likely to identify as air pollution. Such particles are emitted into the atmosphere by fires and industrial processes, wind erosion of barren land, and the exhausts of diesel trucks and buses, to name only a few of the more significant sources.

In developing Asian countries, particulates are often the first form of atmospheric pollution to attract public attention, probably because they are esthetically displeasing, dirtying clothes and making buildings grimy and unsightly. Sustained exposure to high concentrations can, however, damage animal respiratory systems and pose a threat to human health. Until recently this was thought to be exclusively a problem of urban industrial populations but recent research has revealed that rural women in many Asian countries are exposed to extremely high concentrations of particulates due to the long hours they spend cooking over biomass-fueled stoves in poorly ventilated kitchens (Smith, Aggarwal, and Dave 1983).

On the global scale there is concern that increased levels of particle concentration in the atmosphere in the form of dust and aerosols may affect the heat balance of the earth. The deposition of radioactive particles, such as strontium 90, in the atmosphere by nuclear weapons testing also represents a major ecological hazard, although, fortunately, one largely brought under control by the Test Ban Treaty signed in the early 1960s. The pollution that would result from a major nuclear war would, needless to say, threaten the continued existence of the entire biosphere. Recently, it has been suggested that even a relatively limited nuclear war would so increase the level of suspended particles in the upper atmosphere, both dust thrown up in the explosions and smoke produced by burning cities, as to throw the entire earth into a prolonged "nuclear winter" (Ehrlich et al. 1984).

Gaseous pollutants presently have a much wider ecological impact than particles, affecting rural as well as urban areas. High levels of carbon monoxide, sulfur dioxide, and photochemical smog all threaten the health of urban populations, not only of humans but of other animals and plants as well. Windborne sulfur dioxide, converted by atmospheric moisture into "acid rain" can damage forests hundreds of kilometers from its source. The fluorocarbon gases used as propellants in aerosol sprays may rise into the upper levels of the atmosphere where they chemically break down the ozone layer, raising the threat of increased penetration of biologically deadly ultraviolet radiation to the surface of the earth.

Human activities have already seriously modified the heat balance of urban areas. Numerous studies have revealed that atmospheric temperatures in cities throughout the world are on the average of from three to five degrees Celsius warmer than their rural hinterlands (Lowry 1967). This "heat island" effect, as it is called, is quite pronounced in tropical cities such as Kuala Lumpur where air temperatures in the downtown business area may be as much as 5.6°C higher than in surrounding suburbs (Sham Sani 1979). Most of the increase is explained by the fact that urban structures increase absorption of solar radiation while reduction in area covered by vegetation decreases cooling through transpiration. Some of the excess heat, however, is directly generated by machines and vehicles. As societies become increasingly industrialized, using more and more energy per capita, there is reason to be concerned that emission of waste heat into the atmosphere may begin to affect regional and even global atmospheric temperatures. Fossil fuel-based technology is inherently self-limiting in this regard, but the use of nuclear power, particularly if controllable fusion power technology becomes available, will permit essentially unlimited heat pollution of the atmosphere. The need to limit emission of waste heat, therefore, may be in the long run one of the major checks on the development of more complex social systems with their ever-higher rates of energy consumption.

Pollution of the atmosphere by light and sound also is an issue of some concern, particularly in the urban context. Light pollution is essentially an esthetic problem (except for astronomers) making it impossible for city dwellers to see the constellations, but noise pollution can have serious consequences for human health and well-being. Although an essential means of conveying environmental information both for humans and many other animal species, atmospherically transmitted sound waves, if too numerous or intense, can be harmful to many organisms, causing physical pain, damage to ears, and physiological and psychological disturbances of various kinds.

Sound is a pervasive aspect of all terrestrial ecosystems, playing an important role in information flow between many organisms. Even a quiet spot in the countryside will have a background noise level of 25 decibels (one decibel is the lowest sound level that a person with extremely acute hearing can perceive). A quiet office is at 40 db, the inside of an automobile travelling 50 kilometers per hour is at 70 db, a heavy diesel truck passing seven meters away 90 db, and a jet aircraft taking off 140 db. Permanent impairment of hearing ability results from long-term exposure to levels exceeding 90 db, a level usual in many factories, and often exceeded by rock bands in disco clubs. Noise levels above 50 db can interfere with sleeping, reduce ability to concentrate, and otherwise have undesirable physiological and psychological effects (Taylor 1975).

Noise pollution is primarily an urban problem. In the countryside anthropogenic noise is much less of a concern although sonic booms and other aircraft noises can disturb both people and animals. Wild animals are also often easily frightened by the sounds of normal human activities such as talking or laughter although the effects are usually limited to the immediate vicinity of human settlements.

Water Pollution

The major causes of water pollution include deposition of sediments, organic matter, dissolved chemicals and heavy metals, and heat. All forms may have serious impact on ecosystem stability.

Soil erosion and the consequent deposition of sediments into surface waters has always been a common occurrence as is shown by the vast areas of sedimentary rocks existing today, the evidence of past episodes of erosion in the earth's geological history. Normally, however, such erosion is very gradual since the natural vegetation checks the rate at which runoff occurs. In tropical forests annual loss of soil from hillslopes may not exceed a few hundred kilograms per hectare. Disturbance of the forest cover by logging or agricultural clearance tremendously accelerates the rate of soil erosion, raising losses to several thousands or even tens of thousands of kilograms per hectare per year. This soil is carried into the streams and rivers where it greatly increases the waterborne load of suspended sediments. A river flowing through undisturbed Malaysian rain forest may have as few as 2 parts of sediment per million parts of water compared to 6,000 ppm in deforested catchments (Leigh and Low 1973).

Suspended sediments may significantly alter the suitability of the river as a habitat for aquatic life. Many carnivorous fish are unable to find their prey in murky waters. Bottom-dwelling organisms are often killed by being buried by sediments dropping out of suspension. The gradient of the river and hence its susceptibility to flooding can be profoundly altered by deposition of sediments. Reservoirs and irrigation systems may also become choked with silt, a fate that eventually destroyed the economic base of ancient Mesopotamian civilization (Jacobson and Adams 1958). On the other hand, deposition of sediments on the farm lands of the Nile delta by the annual flooding of the river served to maintain fertility there despite thousands of years of cultivation, another example of how what is considered pollution in one context is beneficial in another (Dale and Carter 1955). In the case of the Nile only about one millimeter of silt was deposited each year whereas the rate of deposition in Mesopotamia was considerably higher, which again demonstrates that pollution is largely a problem of scale.

Deposition of organic matter in waters, while often beneficial to aquatic life in small quantities, can lead to vastly increased biological oxygen demand by decomposers with consequent depletion of dissolved oxygen in the water when occurring on a large scale. Few desirable fish species can live in water having under five parts dissolved oxygen per million although some carp and other "rough" fish can tolerate lower levels. Urban sewage

A Conceptual Framework

and effluents from oil palm mills and other agro-industries are major sources of organic matter in tropical Asian rivers. The deposition of chemicals, particularly nitrogen and phosphorus carried by runoff water from agricultural lands and contained in urban waste discharges, also may contribute to depletion of dissolved oxygen. These nutrients promote the growth of aquatic algae which, after their death, sink to the bottom where they are consumed by microorganisms which also use up available dissolved oxygen in the process.

Numerous dangerous chemicals such as DDT and other pesticides are carried by surface runoff into aquatic ecosystems where they are absorbed into the aquatic food chain and gradually concentrated as they pass from trophic level to trophic level. These pesticides, as well as heavy metals such as lead, cadmium, and mercury, can cause sickness and death in carnivores in the upper links of the food chain, including humans, a hazard that will be discussed at greater length in the section on biological pollution.

Thermal pollution, the increase of water temperature as a result of heat deposition, has in recent years become a major threat to the stability of many aquatic ecosystems. In tropical areas clearing of the forest cover exposes rivers to the direct rays of the sun resulting in increases of several degrees in average water temperature. Use of water for cooling in industrial and power generation plants can also profoundly alter the temperature regime for several kilometers downstream from these facilities. Many of the most desirable food fish are extremely temperature sensitive and are either killed or driven off by higher temperatures. The ability of the water to hold dissolved oxygen also falls as temperature rises, a matter of concern in tropical rivers.

Soil Pollution

Soil, in contrast to air and water, cycles through the biosphere on a geological rather than an annual timescale, making it uniquely vulnerable to pollution. A polluted river or lake may recover in a matter of years once the inflow of pollutants is stopped but pollution of the soil can easily persist for decades or even centuries. Major types of soil pollution include deposition of dust and silt, chemicals, and human artifacts.

Wind- and waterborne sediments are often deposited in large quantities on land surfaces. While such sediments may often enhance productivity of the local ecosystem as is the case with the river-deposited silts in the Nile Delta and the Red River Delta in Vietnam, and also with the wind-deposited "loess" soils of China, they may equally often have destructive impact. Hundreds of thousands of hectares of pasture and farm land on the

Sahelian fringes of the Sahara Desert have been destroyed in recent years by the wind-powered southward expansion of the sand dunes. Similar loss of lands has occurred in the Rajasthan Desert of northwestern India (Eckholm and Brown 1977).

Chemical pollution of soils is also often a serious problem. Irrigation of arid lands may lead to deposition of high concentrations of salts in the surface layers, making the soil toxic to crop plants. Such salinization contributed to the decline of agricultural productivity in ancient Mesopotamia (Jacobson and Adams 1958) and is a major threat in many arid zones of the world today. Pesticide residues can also build up to toxic levels if such chemicals are improperly used. It was at one time feared that the herbicides sprayed over southern Vietnam in such large quantities during the war there would contaminate farm lands for long periods. In most areas, however, the high rainfall washed out such chemicals within a single season, restoring the soil to full productivity. Less fortunately, these herbicide residues were then transported into the surface water where at least one potentially mutagenic component—dioxin—may become sufficiently concentrated as it passes up the aquatic food chain to endanger human health (Committee on Effects of Herbicides 1974).

Pollution of the soil with discarded artifacts is one of the more obvious human impacts on the environment. While the litter and rubbish dumping associated with modern urban civilization are both unsightly and costly to dispose of properly, other anthropogenic deposits may have more significant ecological consequences. In long-settled regions within the Sinitic cultural area, much of the arable land surface may become covered with tombs, reducing the human carrying capacity. One of the major rural reforms carried out by the Chinese Communists after they assumed power in 1949 was the removal of grave sites from cultivable fields. Because regions of Asia falling within the area of Indian influence generally practice cremation, the mortuary monuments left by preceding generations are less of a problem. Unfortunately, however, the high demand for fuel for cremations places heavy stress on forest resources and may accelerate deforestation.

Perhaps the most dangerous form of soil pollution in Asia is wholly a product of twentieth century warfare. Unexploded munitions from World War II and postwar colonial struggles are buried in the soil of many tropical Asian countries (Westing 1984). Plowing in Vietnam can be a distinctly hazardous business with many farmers having been injured or killed in the process. Bombs and shells from World War II are still occasionally uncovered in Malaysia and the Philippines. Perhaps the greatest long-term soil pollution hazard is the storage of highly radioactive

Biological Pollution

If pollution were limited to air, water, and soil components of the ecosystem it would not be a matter of such grave concern, but it is not; it inevitably affects the living components of the ecosystem, including humans. Some of this impact is direct and immediate. Plants and animals exposed to high levels of radiation suffer tissue damage. The lungs of animals which breathe in polluted air are also directly damaged so that urban populations exposed to high levels of noxious gases and particulates show much higher rates of respiratory illness than do rural populations living in areas of cleaner air. Crops planted in soils with excessive salt concentrations wither and die. But the major problem that pollution of air, water and soil poses for ecosystem stability is that pollutants in these mediums are taken up by the living components of the ecosystem and undergo biological concentration as they are passed up through the food chain. DDT, the persistent chlorinated hydrocarbon insecticide used in anti-malarial programs in tropical Asia, provides an excellent example of the way in which biological concentration of pollutants occurs.

In the anti-malaria program, DDT in water or kerosene suspension is sprayed on the walls and ceilings of houses in infected areas. Mosquitoes normally light on these surfaces either before or after biting the human occupants and are killed before they can further spread infection. In Malaysia, where the eradication program has been well implemented, malaria has been almost eliminated over wide areas that were formerly severely infested. The program has had unanticipated side effects, however, especially in East Malaysia. There, the insects that landed on the sprayed walls and thatch roofs were caught and eaten by the small house lizards known locally as "chichaks." The chichaks were in turn eaten by the household cats and the cats frequently died. This led to a great increase in the number of rats in the villages and raised the threat of an outbreak of plague. The government responded to this threat by collecting excess cats in Singapore and parachuting them into the isolated settlements (Conway 1972).

The question is, why did the cats die? They died because they had levels of DDT far above permissible levels in their bodies, and they achieved these levels because they were the top carnivores in a long food chain that caused concentration of what had initially been an environmentally dispersed toxic chemical. Thus, each insect eaten by a chichak had only a minute quantity of DDT in its body, so little as to be totally harmless by itself. But a chichak does not eat just one insect, it must eat dozens of them every day in order to meet its energy and nutrient requirements. The DDT is retained in its fatty tissues resulting in a much higher concentration of DDT than was present in any individual insect. Each cat, of course, eats many chichaks, and absorbs the already concentrated DDT from their tissues into its own body where over a relatively short time lethal levels may be achieved.

The same fate that befell the cats of East Malaysia often awaits humans as well, due to our position as a top carnivore, especially with regard to marine ecosystems. Low levels of pesticides, mercury, and other stable toxic compounds in water are taken up by plankton and then concentrated as they pass up through the long aquatic food chain. DDT that was present in the waters of Long Island Sound at a level of only 0.00005 ppm had a concentration of 0.04 ppm in the plankton, 1.24 ppm in herbivorous fish and 2.07 ppm in the carnivorous fish in the same waters. Fish-eating birds showed levels of up to 75.5 ppm in their tissues, a DDT concentration about one million times greater than that present in the water (Woodwell et al. 1967, 1971). People who eat fish are in the same relative position in the food chain as the birds, so that mother's milk in the United States has been found to contain DDT levels four times the permitted safe levels for interstate shipment of cow's milk.

The human disaster caused by mercury poisoning at Minamata, Japan, has become a world symbol for the dangers of biological concentration of toxic materials. There, a factory producing fertilizers and organic chemicals dumped large quantities of methyl mercury into the waters of the Chisso Bay. The mercury became concentrated through the aquatic food chain and finally was consumed in large quantities by the fish-eating local population. After a few years people began to suffer from a mysterious disease that caused them to have violent fits. Some lost their sight and hearing, many died, and soon babies were being born with severe brain damage due to absorption of mercury through the placenta. Only after hundreds of people had fallen victim to what is now called the "Minamata disease" did the Japanese government take any action to halt the dumping of mercury into the bay. No fish taken from its waters are safe to eat and it may take decades before mercury levels drop back to safe levels.

Many chemicals flowing through the ecosystem, such as mercury or lead, are directly toxic to living organisms; others pose more subtle hazards—they increase the incidence of mutations or induce cancer. Such chemical hazards are immensely difficult to detect, however, because of the indirect nature of their impact and because of the low frequency with which they appear in an affected population. Thus, for example, while it is now almost certain that the build-up of tars in the lungs of cigarette smokers causes them to suffer a higher incidence of lung cancer than nonsmokers, it was only by studying a sample of several hundred thousand individuals that such a causal relationship could be detected. It is now suspected that a wide range of common pesticides and food processing chemicals may also cause cancer or mutations if absorbed in sufficient quantities, but satisfactory proof is lacking.

The proliferation of new chemical compounds represents a major threat to living organisms. Many new artificial compounds are extremely stable and nonbiodegradable, meaning that they are not broken down by normal metabolic processes and may thus undergo biological concentration. It is this unseen biological pollution caused by such chemicals, rather than the merely cosmetic problems of dumping of rubbish and litter, that offers the true threat to the continuing stable functioning of the ecosystems on which the survival of all human social systems depends.

Destruction

Destruction refers to the outright physical elimination of ecosystem components: the killing of animals by hunters, the felling of trees by loggers or land developers, the mining of metals and other nonrenewable resources, etc. From its earliest origins, the human species has played a strong destructive role, initially through hunting and collecting of wild plants, and more recently through forest clearance, strip mining, and other massive actions against the natural landscape.

There has been considerable debate about the impact that primitive hunters may have had on wild game populations. A number of archaeologists (Martin and Wright 1967) have advanced the hypothesis that the ancestors of the American Indians, who first entered the Americas via the Bering Straits land bridge from Asia at the end of the Pleistocene period, were responsible for the extinction of several large herbivore species collectively referred to as "megafauna." These animals, including the woolly mammoth, wild horse, camel, and the giant ground sloth, had all evolved in an ecosystem free of the presence of human hunters and, therefore, were presumably not adapted to the presence of humans in their environment, unlike the African megafauna (elephants, antelope, rhinoceros, etc.) which had coevolved with humans since their first appearance on the savannahs some millions of years earlier. Certainly, campsites of early peoples in America display immense quantities of animal bones, indicating that these ancient hunters were efficient predators, although one of their favorite victims, the American bison, far from dying out, continued to wander the Great Plains in huge herds up until the 1880s.

Over-hunting does seem to have led to the extinction of the moas, the giant flightless birds that inhabited New Zealand until recent centuries. Given their lack of either effective means of defense or escape and their low level of intelligence, the moas were easily killed by the Polynesians who first settled New Zealand only a thousand or so years ago (Cumberland 1963). The Polynesians who first settled the Hawaiian Islands may have been responsible for extinction of over half of the endemic bird species. Both direct human predation and habitat modification contributed to this massive rate of extinction which compares to a fifteen percent species loss in the post-Contact period (Olson and James 1982). Other cases of animal extinction attributed to primitive hunters are more problematical, however. The archaeologist, Tom Harrisson (1969-70), has claimed that early hunters in Borneo were responsible for extinction of the tapir and the rhinoceros, but the zoologist, Lord Medway (1977), holds habitat change following the end of the Ice Age responsible. In Peninsular Malaysia, the aborigines may have drastically reduced the number of wild cattle, tapir, and rhinoceros, but only after introduction of firearms vastly increased the firepower of the hunters whose traditional blowpipes and bows had been much less effective weapons (Rambo 1978).

The rate of extinction of wild animals due to human activity has certainly dramatically increased in the past century, reflecting the greater efficiency of weapons, the vast increase in the numbers of hunters, and, most important of all, the widespread disruption of natural habitats as a consequence of agricultural and industrial development. Over one-half of animal species known to have become extinct during the last 2000 years have been lost since 1900 with an average of one species now becoming extinct each year and with at least 1000 additional species considered to be endangered (Eckholm 1978). At present in tropical Asia the elephant, rhinoceros, gaur, serow or wild goat, tiger, orangutan, gibbon, giant panda, and horn-bill, just to mention a few of the more prominent species, are facing imminent extinction. In some cases, such as the rhinoceros, whose horn is highly valued by the Chinese for medicinal purposes, commercial poaching is a direct cause of population decline. Other species, such as the orangutan of Borneo and Sumatra, are avidly pursued for sale to zoos and private collectors. Hunting for meat by tribal and peasant populations also strongly affects many animal populations and may lead to their local destruction. According to one estimate, more than 132,000 wild pigs were killed by hunters in Peninsular Malaysia in 1971 alone (Yong 1979). The major threat to the survival of most of these endangered species, however, is disruption of their habitat as the tropical rain forest is cleared for agricultural use.

As many as 30,000 wild plant species are considered dangerously rare or under immediate threat of extinction with an estimated one species per day being lost in tropical forests alone. Indiscriminate logging and over-exploitation of commercially valuable medicinal and ornamental plants, such as wild orchids, threatens many species. Malaysian aborigines, encouraged by the high prices offered by cane furniture manufacturers, are rapidly sweeping the forests clean of rattan due to their practice of harvesting the cane before it matures and sets the seed necessary to ensure reproduction of the next generation.

Clearance of forest land is the main threat to most tropical plant species. In Peninsular Malaysia more than one million hectares of forest land were converted to agricultural use during the past ten years. Similar rates of clearance are occurring in Thailand, Vietnam, and the outer islands of Indonesia. In Papua New Guinea, Japanese chipboard-making firms are converting forest lands into virtual deserts by stripping off every vestige of vegetation, removing from the ecosystem in the process most of the nutrients necessary for plant regeneration. The vast areas of alluvial land in Malaysia where tin mining has been carried out are also sterile wastelands where not even *Imperata* grass can grow in the toxic sands left on the surface by the dredges.

Accompanying the increased rate of extinction of wild plants has been a dramatic rise in the loss of traditional domestic plant varieties in the years since the launching of the "green revolution" employing genetically standardized high-yielding varieties (National Research Council 1972). In Asia there were literally thousands of distinct varieties of rice in cultivation with each community having its own special types adapted to local conditions. As many as ninety separate named varieties have been reported for a single village in the Philippines while similar diversity was common throughout the region. Since the International Rice Research Institute first introduced its high yielding "miracle" varieties in the early 1960s, they have displaced native varieties in nearly forty percent of the sown area in tropical Asia (Chang 1984). This substitution of a few genetically uniform strains for thousands of local varieties increases the vulnerability of the rice crop to epidemic outbreaks of diseases and insect pests. Whereas traditionally, the spread of disease and insects was inhibited by the great diversity among different types of rice, so that no single pest was likely to be well adapted to more than a small percentage of available varieties, the planting of vast areas with only a single variety offers a splendid evolutionary opportunity to pest and disease species (Conway and McCauley 1983).

Loss of genetic resources is perhaps the single greatest threat to ecosystem stability. Such loss is irreversible—species that have taken millions of years to evolve can be wiped out almost overnight and there is no known way that they can be recreated. Yet the ecological significance of these organisms is often unknown. In fact, probably no more than between fifteen and fifty percent of the species currently in existence have even been given a scientific name, let alone studied in depth. Many still unknown species may have important economic, medical, and scientific potential, much as the cinchona bush, an undistinguished-looking shrub of tropical America, proved to be the source of quinine, the first effective anti-malarial drug, and some seemingly useless molds were the source of the antibiotic drug penicillin. Considering that there still may be many valuable species awaiting discovery, the only sensible policy is one of ensuring maximum possible conservation of remaining natural ecosystems. The saving of such areas, however, in the face of increasing human populations with their need for agricultural land and other resources, is one of the major challenges facing tropical Asia.

Accompanying the destruction of biotic resources is the degradation of the soil component of the ecosystem. Clearance of forests in mountain areas leads to massive soil erosion with consequent loss of productivity. Such destruction is not new. The Greeks and Romans created vast semi-deserts in what had formerly been forested lands in Greece and North Africa. Similar misuse led to the loss of topsoil from huge areas in China and India during the past two thousand years. Growing population pressure in the lowlands, which pushes more and more people into the ecologically fragile upland areas, has vastly increased the rate of land destruction throughout tropical Asia since 1945. Large areas of northern and eastern India, Java, Luzon, and northern Thailand, that were formerly forested hills, have come to resemble the gullied surface of the moon as a result of soil erosion.

Subsurface mineral resources are also being consumed at an ever increasing rate. Known deposits of many minerals such as lead, tin, phosphate, and, of course, petroleum, are quite limited and once used up cannot be replaced. Given the absolute dependence of industrial society on such materials, exhaustion of supplies threatens the continued ability of complex social systems to function effectively.

Disruption

Less dramatic than the outright destruction of components of an ecosystem is the subtle disruption of its structure and functioning as a consequence of human activities. Construction of the Aswan High Dam in Egypt, for example, by blocking the free flow of the Nile, stopped the annual deposition of silt on the downstream fields of the delta causing a long-term fall in their fertility. Cutting off the flow of silt into the Mediterranean Sea has also caused a great decline in the sardine population which subsisted on nutrients carried into the coastal waters by the Nile (Farvar and Milton 1972).

For shy forest animals the mere presence of people in their habitat has a disruptive impact sufficient to prevent their successful reproduction. This vulnerability of large mammals to disruption of their ecosystems is illustrated by the fate of the herd of Sumatran rhinoceros in the Endau-Rompin forest area in Peninsular Malaysia. The Pahang State government allowed loggers to fell timber in the middle of the home range of these rare forest herbivores. Frightened by the noise and activity associated with the timber cutting, the animals fled the area, splitting the herd in the process into several widely scattered remnants which are nonviable breeding units.

Human disruption of natural ecosystems is certainly not a new phenomenon. Early peoples used fire to modify their habitat in ways more favorable to their survival. There is ample evidence that primitive hunting populations in North America, Africa, and Australia deliberately set fire to large areas in their territories each year in order to destroy old tough shrubs and grasses and promote the growth of fresh green shoots to serve as fodder for the wild herbivorous animals that they hunted (Lewis 1972, 1973; O. C. Steward 1956). So systematic is this planned disruption of the natural ecosystem that one Australian anthropologist has labeled it "fire-stick farming" (Jones 1969).

The practice of agriculture is, of course, merely an extreme form of human disruption of natural ecosystems in which human activity alters conditions so as to favor the growth of crop plants while inhibiting the growth of weed species (Hutterer 1983). In swidden farming the cutting of trees reroutes the flow of solar energy from the forest canopy to crops planted at ground level; the burning of the natural vegetation transfers the nutrients stored in the biomass to the soil surface where they are readily available to the crop plants; the heat from the fire destroys weeds and other pests; and the breaking up of the soil surface with digging sticks creates the space necessary for the crop plants to take root so that they can take advantage of the newly available energy and nutrient supplies (Rambo 1980a).

Human disruption of natural ecosystems, therefore, is not necessarily a "bad" thing—it is, in fact, a prerequisite for our survival. It is essential, however, that human activities be so regulated as not to result in the ultimate destruction of the long-term stability and productivity of the biosphere. In particular, it is necessary to maintain at least some natural ecosystems in relatively undisturbed state so that their resources will be available to future generations.

Dissemination

Humans have often been responsible, either deliberately or inadvertently, for the spreading of alien species into new environments (Bates 1956; Elton 1958; Ridley 1930). Primitive tribes brought dogs with them in the course of their migrations into the Americas, Southeast Asia, and Australia. Chickens, pigs, and rats were carried along in their canoes by the ancient Polynesians on their voyages to the Pacific Islands. More recently European ships brought goats and other herbivores to these islands where they have since become naturalized.

The introduction of new species into ecosystems where they have no natural enemies often leads to dramatic population explosions. This has occurred in the case of the rabbit in Australia, the starling and house sparrow in North America, and the African land snail in India and Southeast Asia. At present, house crows, first introduced to Malaysia from India about seventy years ago, are undergoing such an explosion, having spread from Klang to Kuala Lumpur in just five years. In Kuala Lumpur they have found an ideal habitat with abundant food supplies and few competitors or enemies.

Island ecosystems may be particularly vulnerable to disruption by the introduction of alien species (Fosberg 1963). Island plants and animals, because of the isolation in which they have evolved, generally have less developed competitive ability and fewer defenses against predation than do mainland species. When the latter are disseminated into island ecosystems they either kill off or outbreed the unprepared native forms. In Hawaii native species of ground nesting birds, such as the Nene geese, have been virtually driven into extinction by depredations of the introduced rat while the native lowland flora has also been almost wholly displaced by plant colonists, such as the "koa haole" tree (*Leucaena* sp.), which were introduced from Central America in the last century by European visitors. The Hawaiian ecosystem today is almost wholly made up of new components, with little resemblance to its composition when Captain Cook first visited.

Crop plants, particularly, have been the focus of dissemination (Anderson 1967). Within a century of the European discovery of the New World, crops of the American tropics such as maize, manioc, sweet potatoes, chili peppers, pineapple, papaya, and tomatoes had diffused to Africa and Asia, where their introduction resulted in a veritable second agricultural revolution, allowing tremendous intensification of Old World tropical agriculture. Old World grain crops such as wheat, barley, oats and rice, in turn proved equally successful in the Americas, as well as Australia, with the result that Canada, the United States, Argentina, and Australia now supply grain to much of the Old World's population.

Frequently accompanying the deliberate spread of domesticates has been the accidental dissemination of their diseases and pests which, after naturalization, have all too often shifted their attention to more vulnerable native species. Native American chestnut trees, for example, were virtually destroyed by a blight carried on the roots of planting stock of the Chinese chestnut. The diseases that afflict humans have proven particularly able to travel successfully. The native American Indian population was decimated by smallpox and measles carried by the European explorers. The Indians, lacking any acquired resistance to these diseases, suffered huge epidemics which killed off up to ninety percent of their numbers in the space of a hundred years. The Spanish conquest of the Aztecs, often attributed to their superior weapons and organization, may have been as much or more due to the fact that smallpox killed off the cream of the Indian warriors before battle was ever joined. As recently as the 1920s, a vast pandemic of influenza spread throughout the world, killing as many as 100 million people, more than all the casualties in both world wars combined (McNeill 1979).

The development of space travel raises new dangers of ecologically undesirable dissemination, both the carrying of earthly organisms to extraterrestrial environments, and the transporting by returning craft of alien organisms into the biosphere of Earth. By international treaty, all spacecraft must now undergo thorough sterilization to block the unintended seeding of other planets with terrestrial forms. The American astronauts were also subject to quarantine after their return from the moon for fear that they might have contracted alien diseases that would be as devastating to modern human population as smallpox was to the American Indians.

Conclusion

The range of human impacts on the environment is very large. All ecosystem components, including the atmosphere, soil, and water, as well as living organisms, may be affected by human activities. Moreover, the ecological scale at which these effects are felt may range from the destruction of local populations as the result of over-exploitation or habitat disruption on the one hand, to total destruction of the biosphere as a consequence of nuclear war, on the other. The nature of such impacts is likely to vary according to the size and character of each particular social system, and its specific relationships with the ecosystem. In the next chapter, the Semang social system is described and its interactions with the Malaysian tropical rain forest ecosystem examined.

3
The Semang and Their Ecosystem

Scattered about Southeast Asia are small groups of nomadic people who still live by hunting, fishing, and gathering of wild products. These groups, generally referred to as hunters and gatherers, include the Semang or Negritos of Peninsular Malaysia and southern Thailand, the Punan of Borneo, the Mra-Bri or Phi Tong Luang of northern Thailand, the Ruoc and Ta-Cui of Vietnam, the Saoch of Cambodia, the Aeta and the Tasaday of the Philippines, the Kubu of Sumatra, the Shom Pen of the Nicobar Islands, and the Negrito populations of the Andaman Islands.

It is likely that these groups have many different origins and in no sense constitute the scattered remnants of a single, common Paleolithic hunting and gathering culture as was formerly believed by many ethnologists. These groups do, however, share a common mode of ecological adaptation based on hunting and gathering and consequently display many social and cultural characteristics typifying the conventional anthropological conception of a primitive society. They are, in Murdock's (1934) usage, "our primitive contemporaries": people who continue today to follow a way of life in many ways similar to that lived by all humans at an earlier stage of cultural evolution.

All societies in Southeast Asia were similarly dependent on hunting and gathering of wild foods for their subsistence until the development of agriculture. These prehistoric groups, however, are known only from very limited archaeological evidence. *Homo erectus* appeared some 600,000 years ago, but virtually nothing is known about its interactions with the environment.

It was in the late Pleistocene that *Homo sapiens* appeared in Southeast Asia. In fact, the earliest known fossil skull of *Homo sapiens* yet found anywhere in the world was dug up from deposits in Niah Cave, Sarawak, which have an estimated age of 39,600 B.C. Animal bones found in the same site show that by this date humans were already accomplished hunters, successful in killing a wide range of forest animals (see Hutterer, 1977, for a useful review of Southeast Asian Paleolithic archaeology).

The earliest hunters and gatherers of whom there is detailed information are the so-called Hoabinhian cultures of the Late Pleistocene–Early Holocene (40,000 B.P. to 5,000 B.P.). More than twenty Hoabinhian sites have been excavated so far in Indochina, Thailand, Peninsular Malaysia and Sumatra. Most of these sites are in rockshelters in upland areas near small streams while a smaller number are open air coastal sites. Those sites that have been carefully excavated show stone hand axes and scrapers chipped from water rounded pebbles, sharp flakes with signs of edge wear, and, in upper layers, crude cord-marked pottery. Plant remains have been inadequately studied but a wide variety of faunal remains are reported including bones of wild pigs, rhinoceros, goats, deer, several species of primates, squirrels, mice and rats, porcupines, bears, bats, tortoises, reptiles, birds, snails, molluscs, and fish. Charcoal, primarily derived from bamboo, is present in large quantities (Gorman 1971).

No remains of shelters have been found outdoors. The rockshelter sites, however, appear to have been occupied only sporadically rather than continuously, which would be the pattern expected with a hunting and gathering population.

Nothing is known about the social organization of the Hoabinhian people although they probably lived in small groups as the living area in most of the cave sites is very limited. The surviving stone tools are quite crude and show only a few basic patterns which might suggest a very restricted cultural inventory but it has been suggested that bamboo and wood, which do not survive in the archaeological deposits, were used to make a much greater variety of implements (Hutterer 1976, 1977). That so much bamboo charcoal is found and that all of the animal bones are cut into very small, generally uncharred fragments suggests that green bamboo tubes were used for cooking pots just as is done by modern Semang nomads (Gorman 1971). Marking of pottery with cord impressions is evidence that cord was made which could also have been used for fishing nets, bow strings, and carrying bags, although no direct evidence of such artifacts survives.

The Hoabinhian populations appear to have been "broad spectrum" hunters and gatherers who made use of a very wide variety of plants and animals. Such a resource exploitation pattern requires a very detailed knowledge of the environment, particularly of edible plants. Such knowledge is probably a necessary precondition for the development of agriculture, a cultural advance that appears to have spontaneously occurred among the Hoabinhian groups in northern Thailand some 5000 to 7000 or more years ago (Solheim 1972).

The development of agriculture caused a profound change in the environment of Southeast Asian hunters and gatherers. Some groups gradually shifted into being full-time agriculturalists while other groups remained foragers but now occupying a much modified ecosystem where food could be obtained in exchange for forest products by trading with settled agricultural populations. Most, if not all, modern hunters and gatherers in Southeast Asia, with the sole exception of the Andaman Islanders, are involved in such trade relations to the point where it is doubtful that they could survive if trade were cut off. The Semang are especially heavily dependent on such commercial relations so that, although they are "primitive" in the sense of having a small scale social system and a simple, low energy technology, they are in no sense an isolated, wholly autonomous cultural group. Instead, they are incorporated into a larger "world system," to use Wallerstein's (1980) terminology, in which they are specialists in collection of natural resources from the tropical rain forest to meet the needs of other more developed societies. Thus, the Semang are primitive, not because they have failed to evolve, as was believed by ethnologists such as Schebesta (1973) and Cooper (1940), but because the niche they occupy in the modern world system enjoins such a sociocultural status on its occupants. To borrow Richard Fox's (1969) very apt label for similar groups in the Indian subcontinent, these modern Southeast Asian hunters and gatherers are best understood as being "professional primitives."

An Ethnographic Introduction to the Semang*

The lowland forests of northern Peninsular Malaysia and southern Thailand are the home of many small groups of nomadic forest foragers. In the ethnographic literature they are usually referred to as "Semang" although they do not know or use this name themselves, calling themselves instead either after their language group, e.g., Jahai, Mendrik, Lanoh, or by a term, such as *menrat* in Jahai, which means "people." The Department

---

* Although the least numerous of the Malayan aboriginal groups, the Semang have attracted a disproportionate share of attention from ethnographers. Standard published accounts are those of Carey (1976), Endicott (1979), Evans (1937), and, above all, Schebesta (1952, 1954, 1957, 1973). In writing this section I have drawn heavily on these standard sources as well as field observations by my students from the University of Malaya and myself.

of Aboriginal Affairs of Malaysia now officially labels them "Negritos" because many are short and very dark skinned. From a scientific standpoint, however, application of a racial term to a cultural category is undesirable since, as anthropologists have recognized since at least the time of Boas, race, language, culture, and ecological adaptation are not necessarily covariant. Many individual members of Semang bands do not have the physical attributes associated with "Negritos" while many Temiar and Semai swidden agriculturalists display Negrito racial characteristics. Hence, in the present work, Semang will be used for lack of a better substitute.

It is generally estimated that there are at present somewhere between two and three thousand Semang (Carey 1976). This may represent some recent decrease in numbers due to epidemics and loss of territory to other ethnic groups but their total population was probably never very much larger than it is today.

The Semang, if one employs the evolutionary typologies of Julian Steward (1955) and Elman Service (1962), represent the band level of sociocultural integration. Bands are the simplest, least internally differentiated societies known in the ethnographic record. It is this sociocultural simplicity, rather than any pejorative assessment of their mental capability, that justifies referring to the Semang as "primitive."

Descriptions of band-level societies are often phrased in the negative, listing all of the institutions of "civilized" societies that they lack, such as courts, police and armies, religious hierarchies, hereditary rulers, class stratification, slavery, etc. Kinship is the principal means of integration in band societies. Band members assist one another and cooperate together because they are kinspeople and as such they owe certain obligations to each other. There are no specialized institutions that can compel people to fulfill their social obligations. Individual Semang act only because they want to and they want to because they have been socialized in family units where they have learned to behave towards certain classes of relatives in certain manners. A Jahai Semang man, for example, must avoid close contact with his mother-in-law. Such mother-in-law avoidance seems to be functionally associated with the tendency towards patrilocal postmarital residence where men take wives from other bands and bring them to live in their own father's band. Patrilocal residence tends, of course, to create a situation where all the adult males in a band are fathers and sons or brothers while all of the women are unrelated having come from diverse other bands. Having grown up together and knowing their own territory for all their lives, the men are better able to engage in cooperative hunting than would a group of men who were strangers to each other and to the band territory until adulthood, as tends to be the case with groups following a matrilocal rule of postmarital residence.

Among the Semang, descent is bilateral, i.e., a child is considered to be equally related to both its mother and her kindred and the father and his kindred (Abdul Rashid 1976). Bilateral systems are found in all the other hunting and gathering bands in the region including the Aeta and the Andamanese. It seems likely that in the case of tropical forest foragers where men and women contribute about equally to subsistence and where hunting is mainly of small, nondangerous game, there is no great advantage to rigid patrilocal-patrilineal band structure. According to Gomes (1979:90), sixty-six percent of marriages among the Rual Semang were band exogamous. Of these, seventy percent were patrilocal.

Each Semang band wanders inside of a loosely defined territory referred to as a *saka,* having an area of from 100 to perhaps 300 square kilometers. The Semang in modern times make no attempt to defend their territory. If Malays or other outsiders migrate into the area and settle on Semang territory, the latter simply withdraw deeper into the forest. It may have been that in past times, before the power differential between the aborigines and the Malays became so great, the Semang did try to forcibly defend their territories as there are reports of Semang bowmen being involved in wars in the pre-colonial period.

Other attributes of the Semang social system which justify designating it as primitive include: (1) a small population, (2) a very limited degree of division of labor and role specialization, (3) a small cultural inventory, (4) a limited supply of energy, and (5) a simple and low power technology.

Small Population Size

Semang bands usually number less than fifty members. The six bands at Sungai Rual, for example, range from 17 to 49 members with a mean of 31 people per band (Gomes 1982).

Many members of any band are children, however, so that the number of functioning adults may be quite small. In the Sungai Rual groups, nearly two-fifths of their members are below the age of fourteen and half are under twenty years. In the smallest band there are only nine adults out of seventeen people (Gomes 1976:24-29). This paucity of personnel places a low limit on the extent of role specialization possible within the social system.

Limited Role Specialization

Division of labor within a band is based almost entirely upon age and sex. Children contribute little to the economic life of the band until they reach late adolescence. However, even when still quite young they begin to imitate the economic activities of adults. For example, I have observed a group of boys and girls constructing a small shelter of their own, catching fish and gathering wild plants, and then cooking and eating the food together, all copying in miniature what they have seen their parents do many times before. In this manner, with no formal schooling, they are gradually prepared to take on the roles that they will fill when they reach maturity.

The major division of labor is between the sexes. Men are the hunters, collectors of plant products that require tree climbing or other risky activity, the sole users of fish nets and spear-guns, and the decision-makers about future band activities and movements. Women care for the children, cook and do most domestic chores (carrying of water, gathering of firewood), build the shelters, and gather terrestrial food plants such as wild yams. Women also fish.

Sexual division of labor, although clearly demarcated, is not rigidly enforced nor is it reinforced by strong religious taboos as is frequently the case in primitive societies. Specialization is essentially pragmatic. Women, who are of smaller stature than men, and who are in any case frequently restricted in their freedom of movement by pregnancy or the carrying of an infant, specialize in those jobs that require less rapid movement and less muscular strength than the jobs done by the men. There is little concern felt about doing jobs normally reserved for members of the opposite sex, however, so that if a man's wife is sick he will not hesitate to tend the baby or bring the water to the camp. Similarly, I have seen women carrying their husbands' blowpipes when a band is shifting camp from one site to another.

The only real specialist roles in Semang society are those of the band headman and the shaman, or ritual curer *(halak)*. Each band has a headman, a mature male who is respected for his good judgment and high level of competence. Often the position is inherited from father to son but this is only true if the son shares his father's leadership qualities. An incompetent headman will quickly lose his following as band members slip off to join other, better-led groups. In any case, even the most respected headman has few powers or privileges. He must do all the normal work of a Semang male plus provide leadership to the other members of his group. His reward is solely measured in terms of increased prestige rather than the gaining of any economic advantage. His real power is negligible as he can only lead by example, having no power to enforce his will on others. Usually, of course, people follow the lead of the headman, not out of fear or respect for his rank, but because he is known as the most skillful hunter and forager in the group and therefore it is to their own immediate advantage to accept his advice.

The *halak* also tends to be hereditary with a son learning the esoteric curing knowledge from his father. This is not always the case, however, and any young man who has the appropriate dreams of meeting the tiger spirit can apprentice himself to an experienced practitioner and learn the craft. As in the case of the headman, being the *halak* brings extra responsibilities and obligations but few material rewards to the person filling the role. In fact, *halak* often try to hide the fact that they are shamans and enjoy no special prestige in their communities as a result of their skills.

Small Cultural Inventory

The total cultural inventory of the Semang is an extremely small one, so that a single Semang can, in the course of a lifetime, come to know it in its entirety. The precise size of Semang cultural inventory is unknown but their material culture includes a total of fewer than 200 traits,* of which, approximately ten percent are recent borrowings from neighboring agricultural societies.

Limited Supplies of Energy

According to Leslie White's (1943) views on the relationship between energy and cultural evolution, the "primitive" character of the Semang social system is a reflection of their very low ability to capture and utilize energy. The Semang are almost wholly dependent on human muscle power for performing the work necessary to make their social system function. The only significant domestic animal is the dog which is occasionally used in hunting wild pigs and which also helps guard their camps against wild animals. Fire utilizes the energy stored in wood for purposes of cooking and for changing the microclimate of the shelter. Smoke generated by the

---

* A count was made of all of the material cultural traits mentioned in Evans' (1937) comprehensive monograph, *The Negritos of Malaya*. Using even the most generous definition of what constitutes a separate trait, e.g., counting a bow string as a distinct item from a bow, it was possible to list only 167 separate traits, of which 21 are clearly recent introductions and 146 are indigenous for some hundreds of years at least. The author can list an additional twenty or so traits that Evans does not mention, but only one, the stone used for sharpening knives, has any antiquity in Semang culture. Evans probably also under-reports medicines, which might swell the trait list to twice its present size.

fire also helps keep mosquitoes out of the shelter. Usually, a small fire smolders around the clock next to each sleeping platform so that in a single circular shelter there may be as many as seven or eight fires burning at once. Each nuclear family maintains a separate fire and is responsible for obtaining fuel for it.

The Semang also employ fire to clear litter from wild bamboo groves in the forest, making it easier to get at the stalks to harvest them and, in the process, also promoting the growth of new shoots. Although conceptually similar to the "fire stick farming" described by Jones (1969) for the Australian aborigines, the scale of such deliberate environmental modification among the Semang is very much lower and the energy involved is insignificant in total caloric terms. Fire is also used to clear fields in their sporadic attempts to practice swidden farming. Such use of biomass energy may reach very major levels among other Malayan aboriginal groups (Rambo 1982b), but does not constitute an important factor in Semang energetics.

Water power, in the form of rivers flowing from the mountains to the sea, is used to move bamboo rafts carrying rattan and other forests products. Only some Semang groups have access to suitable navigable rivers, however, and even among these groups rafting is a quite infrequent event so that its contribution to their energy budget is probably very small.

The total average per capita daily consumption of energy among the Semang probably does not exceed 5,000 kilocalories of which 40 percent is derived from human labor and 60 percent from the burning of firewood in their cooking and shelter fires. In comparison, average daily per capita energy consumption in the United States is around 250,000 kilocalories (Cook 1971). The Semang, therefore, definitely can be assigned to the low end of the energy use spectrum.

Low-powered Technology

Not only are the Semang a low energy society but their traditional technology does not significantly multiply the small supply of energy available to them. Only a very few tools are used. Knives and, to a much lesser degree, axes, are the principal tools used in the making of other tools. The *parang* is a bush knife of highly generalized design which can be used to perform a multitude of tasks from clearing a swidden field to shaving the head, in fact for all tasks that require cutting. Because it is a general purpose instrument, however, it is not a notably efficient one for doing any particular task.

The digging stick, carved on the spot from any convenient sapling, is the main tool used in the collection of tubers and also for digging wild animals such as bamboo rats out of their dens. It performs effectively only in moist soft forest soils but requires expenditure of a great deal of energy to shift a small amount of dirt. Unlike the *cangkol* hoe used by Malay peasants, the digging stick makes no use of leverage to increase force delivered at the cutting edge.

The blowpipe is a marvelously efficient user of the limited force generated by the human lung. The propelling power is so weak, however, that only a very light projectile can be fired at low velocity over a short distance. Hence the striking force of the dart is insufficient to kill even the smallest game on impact either by its shock or by making a deep wound with serious internal damage. It is only because its darts carry *ipoh* poison that the blowpipe is able to kill even small animals. The bow, which was formerly used by the Semang, was a much more powerful weapon. Because the Semang did not properly fletch their arrows, accuracy was poor, although animals as large as rhinoceros could be killed. Early in the colonial period, the bow was abandoned, probably because firearms, which had greater accuracy and killing power, became available (Rambo 1978). Adoption of firearms, however, made the Semang dependent on external sources of energy supply in the continuing need for powder. This was expensive and often difficult to obtain, making firearms of only secondary significance as weapons in comparison to blowpipes.

Traps are only rarely employed by the Semang who admit that neighboring Senoi swidden farmers are much more skillful in their construction. In any case, spear traps are dependent on human muscle power for their operation although some snares and pit traps rely on energy provided by the animal itself. The great advantage of traps from an energy standpoint is their automatic operation which in effect multiplies the area and time span that a human hunter can cover effectively.

Except for the rare use of current-powered rafts, all transportation is dependent on human muscle power with walking and running on foot the only means of movement. Loads are carried in small woven backpack bags. These bags have such narrow shoulder straps that they can only be comfortably used to carry light loads over relatively short distances. Infants are generally carried astride the mother's hip supported in a cloth sling. Lack of more adequate load-carrying equipment is certainly a limiting factor on the size of Semang cultural inventory.

Given such limited availability of energy supplies and simple, low-powered technology, the Semang social system would not be a complex one even in a very rich environment. The Semang ecosystem, however, is not a rich one. It is characterized by scarce and widely dispersed resources which become available on a highly irregular basis.

The Semang Ecosystem

The picture of the Semang presented in many ethnographic accounts is that of a people dwelling deep in the jungle, living their traditional hunting and gathering way of life in splendid isolation from the outside world. This picture is a false one as the Semang are much more in contact with their "civilized" neighbors than are many of the more culturally complex Senoi groups. Unlike the Senoi, the Semang do not inhabit the remote interior mountains of the Main Range. Instead, they live in the more readily accessible coastal foothills and inland river valleys. The elevation seldom exceeds 200 meters in contrast to the Senoi who are often found at elevations exceeding 1,000 meters. Nor are the Semang people of the deep jungle. Most groups have their territories close to the fringe of the forest where they are in close contact with Malay farmers and Chinese shopkeepers. This places the Semang in position to exploit the resources of what ecologists refer to as an ecotone, a transitional zone between two major biotic communities where plants and animals tend to be particularly diverse. The Semang have access both to the wild plants and animals of the forest and to the opportunities for trade and wage labor presented by the settled farming communities. The spectrum of resources available to them is consequently far wider than it is for populations living either deep in the forest or wholly in the agricultural zone. Their whole social system, as Geoffrey Benjamin (1973) has observed, can be seen as being adapted to opportunistic exploitation of this very diverse and rapidly changing resource base.

The Semang ecosystem is presented in schematic form in Figure 3. It includes four major components: the forest, the river, the swidden field *(ladang),* and the Malay village *(kampung).* The Semang social system interacts with each of these components in ways described in detail below.

The Forest

However rich the Malayan rain forest may appear to the outside observer, it is a virtual desert from the standpoint of the hunter and gatherer living under its thick canopy. Game animals and edible wild plants are scarce and widely scattered. In certain seasons even experienced jungle travelers may go hungry in less favored areas. This paucity of food supplies suitable for human consumption reflects the vegetative structure of the primary rain forest. The giant trees form a dense canopy which cuts off virtually all sunlight from the floor of the forest. At ground level the forest is in a perpetual state of gloom. Even on a bright sunny day, photography

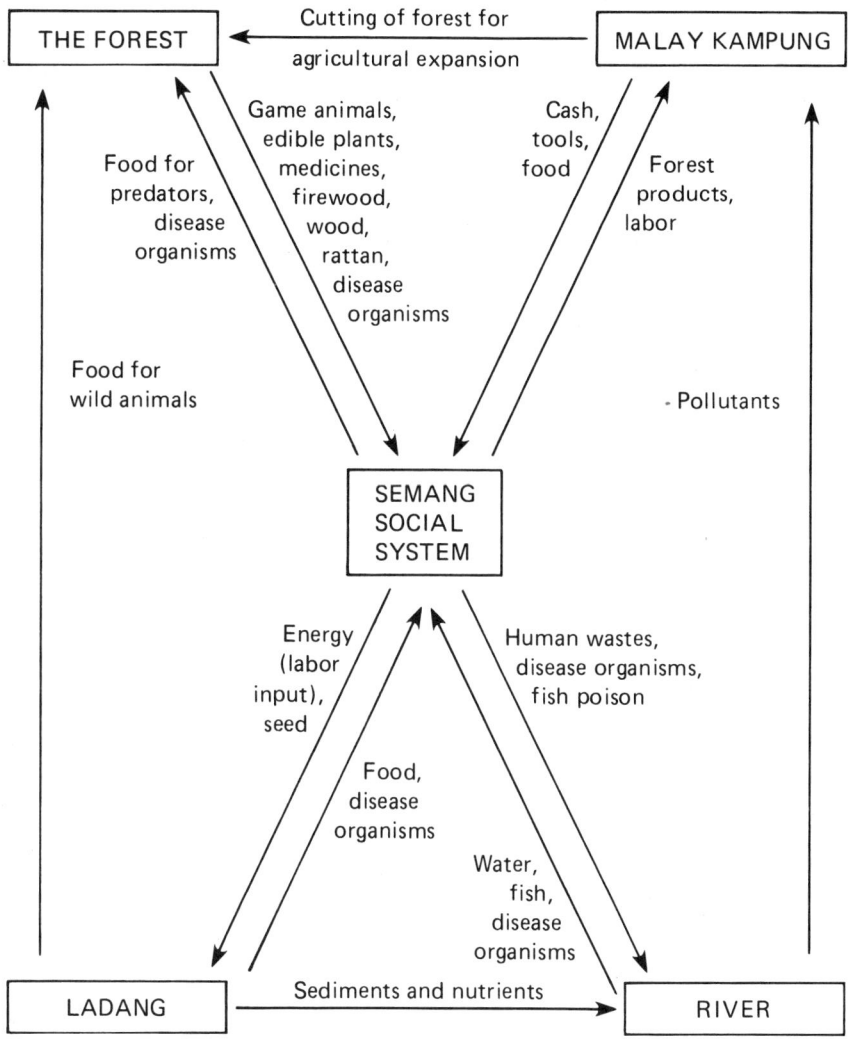

Figure 3. The Semang in relation to their ecosystem.

on the forest floor requires supplementary flash or the use of extremely high speed film. At such reduced light levels, growing conditions are unfavorable for understory plants. As a consequence, the ground surface of true rain forest is quite open and walking is relatively easy, unlike the situation in second growth forest (known in Malay as *belukar*) where one must cut one's way through the dense growth with a bush knife. This openess of the forest floor also means, of course, that few edible plants grow within reach of ground dwelling mammals, which explains the low population densities of wild cattle, wild pig, rhino, tapir, and deer and other herbivores in the deep forest.

Edible leaves and fruits are concentrated in the upper stories of the forest where they support a diverse and abundant fauna including several species of monkeys and squirrels. These arboreal animals, however, are rarely even visible let alone accessible to ground-dwelling predators. It is only the blowpipe that permits the Semang to successfully hunt these tree dwellers.

Edible plants are also a scarce resource at ground level. Wild yams, whose tubers are buried beneath the surface but whose vines climb high into the upper canopy in search of light, are the primary wild source of carbohydrates for the Semang. A wide variety of wild fruit trees are found scattered in the forest and these are avidly exploited by the Semang both for food and to obtain products to sell in the neighboring Malay villages. Wild durian is a mainstay of their diet during the two or three month annual fruit season. Seeds of the leguminous *petai (Parkia speciosa)* and *kerdas (Pithecellobium jiringa)* trees are particularly valuable commodities, with the Semang at Sungai Rual earning more than $1,000 from the sale of *kerdas* alone during the six week fruiting season in 1976.

Other forest plants are sought for use in making artifacts or for trade purposes. Bamboo of various species is used for a multitude of purposes by the Semang. Large stems have their internodes broken out and are used for carrying and storing water. Smaller tubes are used for cooking vessels. Blowpipe tubes are made from a particular rare species *(Bambusa wrayi)* that grows in only a few clumps deep in the Main Range (Noone 1955). Semang from Sungai Rual must walk for three days to reach the site of the one clump known to them.

Rattan is much sought after both for use in their own crafts and for sale to outside dealers. Numerous roots and flowers are collected for sale to the Malays and Chinese as medicine, especially the *Ubi Jogoh* root which is reputed to be a powerful aphrodisiac. Typically, the Semang receive only two dollars per *kati* (one and one-third pounds) from the dealer although it sells on the outside for one dollar per small piece of which there are more than twenty per *kati*. Incense is collected by tapping certain wild trees while, formerly, dammar gum was of very high value although the development of cheaper synthetics has undercut the market. Wild animals, particularly *berok* monkeys, are also sometimes captured when young and raised for sale to the Malays who use them to harvest coconuts.

The forest is also the home of two animals that the Semang greatly fear, the tiger and the elephant. Elephants have been known to trample through campsites and also reputedly delight in tearing up crops in the *ladangs*. On one occasion I set off a panic among the Semang at Sungai Rual when I reported having seen elephant dung in the forest a couple of kilometers from the settlement. Tigers compete with the Semang in hunting game animals and also sometimes kill Semang. The mere presence of a tiger in an area is sufficient grounds for people to move their camp even if they have just set it up. One protective taboo prohibits anyone from walking down a track that another person has just come up as it is believed that the second traveler is likely to meet up with any tiger that might be tracking the first party.

It is in the forest that the Semang encounter the most feared element of their environment, the lightning and thunder storms that they believe are caused by the anger of the deity *Karei*. A storm in the Malaysian forest is truly a terrifying experience with blinding lightning flashes followed immediately by deafening cracks of thunder. The rain falls in heavy sheets while great gusts of wind shake the trees to their roots, often causing some aged giant to fall with a crash. Semang have been killed in the past by falling trees, which adds to the terror they feel whenever the intensity of the storm increases. Their response is to cut their shins and mix their blood with water in a small bamboo tube and then throw this mixture into the air as a pacification offering to *Karei*. Following a particularly severe storm they will invariably shift their camp to a new, and, they hope, safer site.

Along with large predators, the forest is also the habitat of leeches, mosquitoes, and other parasites of the Semang. There is a taboo against killing leeches as it is believed to offend *Karei*. Mosquitoes are thought to be souls of dead people and some Semang will not slap them. Mosquitoes, of course, spread malaria which is one of the most serious diseases affecting the health of the Semang.

The River

Semang campsites are usually located close to a river. The river is their source of drinking water, their bath and laundry, their toilet, their fishing grounds, and sometimes, a transportation route used for drifting rafts loaded with rattan and other forest products to the Malay *kampung* downstream. The river is thus an extremely important component of the Semang ecosystem.

Rivers are generally the most productive parts of tropical rain forest areas. They form an ecotone, a zone where two distinctive communities meet. The course of the river breaks the closed canopy of the forest allowing light to penetrate to the ground surface so that there is an abundant growth of herbaceous plants on the stream banks. Terrestrial mammals are attracted both by this food supply and by their need for drinking water and bathing places. The concentration of plants and animals provides organic food matter for the fish in the river.

The Semang take most of their drinking water from the river although a thirsty hunter in the deep forest may, if no river is convenient, cut lianas and drink the water that drips from the vine. When on the move, people drink directly from the river by scooping up water in a folded leaf. In camp, they bring it to their shelters in long bamboo tubes. When they move to a new site, these tubes are always split open and then laid with hollow side to the ground. It is their belief that if this were not done they would suffer stomach pains but it also eliminates potential breeding sites for mosquitoes.

Because rivers are customarily used for toilet purposes, water is always drawn from the river above the campsite. If other groups are thought to be living upstream then water will be taken only from smaller streams flowing into the main river. This is done because the Semang say they do not want to drink anyone else's feces. Their reasons are esthetic but they serve the practical purpose of protecting them from waterborne disease organisms. Such protection is needed since water is not boiled or otherwise treated before drinking.

The river is also used for bathing and laundry. Most Semang bathe at least once a day but personal cleanliness is not otherwise of great concern and their few clothes are only rarely washed.

Catching of fish and collection of river snails and other aquatic invertebrates is a major concern of the Semang. Fish provided a large part of the protein consumed by the Semang at Sungai Rual. They are caught by tickling by hand under rocks, with bamboo fish traps, and with nets bought from the Malays. Recently, goggles and rubber band-powered spear guns have come into use and have proved highly effective. Derris root and, when it can be obtained from the *kampung* people, chemical insecticide are also sometimes employed to poison fish.

Those groups located near large rivers occasionally will build bamboo rafts and run these downstream carrying their stocks of rattan and other forest products in order to trade these at one of the market towns. Because of the swift current it is a one-way trip for the rafts and the people have to return to their territory on foot. Smaller water courses are often used as trails by the Semang.

The Swidden Field (Ladang)

Although basically nomadic foragers, Semang bands will from time to time clear a small patch of forest and try their hands at farming. They are usually not very successful at this endeavor, however, and agricultural activity provides only a small percentage of their total food. It has often been assumed that farming is a cultural practice that the Semang have only recently borrowed from their more "evolved" Senoi and Malay neighbors, and it is this that explains the generally poor results they obtain (Schebesta 1973). It should be remembered, however, that as jack-of-all-trades opportunistic foragers, the Semang are not particularly skillful at any specific activity, including supposedly more traditional ones such as hunting and trapping. Hence, lack of skill in farming does not serve as convincing evidence that this is a newly borrowed technique. Instead, I agree with Hutterer (1983) that Southeast Asian foragers like the Semang have intermittently practiced agriculture for a very long time. They take it up when the terms of trade are unfavorable for wild forest products and drop it when other opportunities appear more rewarding.

The Semang employ the swidden method of agriculture, which is also known as slash and burn or shifting cultivation. They first use bush knives and axes to cut the trees and bushes in a small hillslope plot (called *ladang* in Malay). After the felled vegetation is sufficiently dry it is set alight and the plot burned over. In comparison to other Orang Asli groups such as the Temiar and Semai, the Semang generally do a poor job of burning and many unburned trunks and stumps are left in the field. No attempt is made to collect these and refire them, so that much of the surface of the plot can not be planted.

After the soil has cooled, maize, manioc (commonly referred to in Malaysia as tapioca), peanuts, and hill rice are planted using a wooden dibble stick to punch holes in the ground. The plot is then left to itself while the people return to their nomadic round of foraging in the forest. When they think the crops are ready for harvest the Semang return to their *ladang*. More often than not they find little food left because the forest animals have already taken their share from the unprotected field. Elephants like to uproot the manioc and crush the other plants while wild pigs also often destroy much of the crop. Despite these losses, the Semang evidently get enough returns from their labor investment to make swiddening worthwhile. It may be that their principal reward comes from better hunting due to the increased number of game animals in the vicinity of the swiddens.

The Malay Village (Kampung)

Ethnographers have generally either ignored the role played by Malays, Chinese and other outsiders in Semang adaptation to their ecosystem or have deplored contacts with these foreign elements as causing culture change and distortion of the "true" Semang way of life (Schebesta 1973). It is becoming increasingly clear, however, that for hundreds and probably thousands of years the Semang have had important relationships with neighboring settled farmers and merchants and thus these groups, which are here lumped together under the short-hand term, the *kampung*, constitute a key component of the Semang ecosystem.

A typical *kampung* on the edge of the forest is the center for a number of diverse activities. Malays, most of whom are petty traders or peasant smallholders engaged in growing of padi and rubber, form the majority population. A few Chinese shopkeepers may also be present. Logging or tin mining companies and their employees may also be based at the *kampung*. There is likely to be a governmental presence in the form of a police post or army camp. The *kampung* is also a transportation and communication center served either by a road or navigable river and generally having telephone or radio connections to the outside.

The *kampung* is primarily of interest to the Semang as a source of food and manufactured commodities. These are obtained either in exchange for forest products collected by the Semang or in return for their services as hired agricultural laborers. A large variety of forest products, particularly rattan, fruits, and medicinal plants, are brought to the *kampung* and sold to the merchants there. Often no cash is paid but the amount simply credited to the account that the individual Semang has with the shop. The lack of mathematical proficiency of the Semang allows unscrupulous dealers to manipulate their account books so that the forest people are in perpetual debt. The merchants also pay very low prices for the forest products which they then resell at a considerable markup after transporting them to the urban markets. The Semang know that they are being taken advantage of but feel helpless to change the situation. Only if a particular merchant takes too gross advantage will they respond by shifting their trade to another, more honest dealer.

The range of commodities obtained through trade is great. The Semang at Sungai Rual were observed to purchase knives, cooking pots, clothing, flashlights and batteries, shotgun shells, matches, kerosene, women's makeup, soap, salt, sugar, bottled soft drinks, sweets, tobacco and cigarettes, tinned sardines, cooking oil, and a variety of other foodstuffs. The major commodity, however, both in terms of weight and value, was rice. Carbohydrate supplies in the forest are so limited in quantity and poor in quality that such external supplements are necessary if the Semang are to survive there.

It is the need to obtain rice that also motivates the Semang to work as temporary laborers on Malay farms. Whole bands will work during the rice harvest in return for a share of the padi or will contract to clear rubber land in return for a daily rice ration. Individual Semang men will also take on temporary work as guides for loggers or other extractive industries in return for wage payments.

Since independence, the Malaysian government has sought to increase the integration of the Semang into the national social and economic system. The Department of Aboriginal Affairs (JOA) has played a key role in this program. Particular emphasis is placed upon providing medical assistance and educational opportunities to the Semang. A JOA officer is stationed in Jeli, the *kampung* closest to Sungai Rual, to work with the Semang resettled there. It is JOA's goal to convert them into settled agriculturalists. The long-term success of this policy is doubtful but in the short-run closer ties have been established between the nomads and the outside world. The *kampung* is becoming an increasingly significant component of the Semang ecosystem.

4
The Impact of the Semang on Their Ecosystem

Preceding chapters have outlined a conceptual framework for studying the impacts that human societies have on the environment, described the Semang social system, and presented a model of its interactions with the Malaysian rain forest ecosystem. The present chapter presents empirical information on specific impacts of the Semang on their ecosystem. The reader will note that available data are tantalizingly incomplete. More questions are raised than can be answered and most findings are suggestive rather than conclusive.

These limitations reflect the conditions under which the study was carried out. Ideally, such an investigation should be conducted by an interdisciplinary team of ecologists and anthropologists. It was not possible to organize such a large scale effort and I was forced to carry out all data collection on my own although I was greatly aided by advice given by colleagues in the natural science departments of the University of Malaya.

Field conditions were also less than optimal. A guerrilla struggle was in progress in the area between the Malayan Communist party and the Malaysian Armed Forces. Because of this, my students and I were unable to accompany the Semang on overnight collecting trips into distant areas and were not able to go outside of the settlement itself after nightfall.

The Semang themselves, although personally friendly, were often difficult informants to work with. As other investigators have noted (Schebesta 1973), they are not systematic thinkers and, unlike other Malaysian aborigines, do not enjoy answering questions about their environmental knowledge (Rambo 1980a). They also were frightened by the presence of scientific instruments in their settlement. Shiny metal objects were thought to attract the attention of *Karei,* the feared god of thunderstorms. Being initially unaware of this, I had set up a weather station, including a bright aluminum evaporation pan, in the center of the settlement. That night the settlement was subjected to a very heavy thunderstorm. Soon several obviously frightened Semang came to my shelter and begged me to dismantle the equipment so that *Karei* would end the storm. I immediately complied and the storm ended, but so did the opportunity to make desired measurements. In the following pages reference will be made to a number of questions that could not be answered because of Semang fears of scientific equipment.

Nevertheless, despite methodological limitations and the constraints imposed by the field situation, a considerable amount of new information was collected on the impact of the Semang on their environment. These data are presented under the appropriate ecosystem components of atmosphere, climate, water, soil, plants, and animals. They are also categorized according to five progressively higher levels of the ecosystem hierarchy at which human–environment interactions may occur: the individual organism's immediate life space, the household or shelter site, the local community or settlement area, the watershed or region, and the biosphere or global level.

The Atmosphere

Given the immense volume of the atmospheric reservoir, it would at first consideration seem unlikely that the activities of primitive people could have any measurable impact on overall air quality. At the global level this is certainly the case but at a more local level the Semang have certainly been responsible for some atmospheric pollution. In fact, the individual Semang may suffer greater exposure to certain air pollutants than does the average citizen in modern industrial society. Atmospheric pollution will be described in terms of gases and particulate matter, disease germs, odors, light, and sound.

Emission of Gases and Particulate Matter

The Semang, like all people, primitive or civilized, engage in respiration twenty-four hours per day. In this process, oxygen is removed from the air and carbon dioxide and water vapor added to it. Given the huge quantity of oxygen in the atmosphere, the rapid mixing of gases, and the very porous construction of their houses, it is unlikely that Semang respiration has any measurable effect on gas concentrations even at the household level.

Gases produced through combustion of wood, kerosene, and tobacco represent a much greater volume including some highly toxic compounds, especially carbon monoxide. It was not possible to obtain quantified measurements of gas and particle concentration but it was observed that houses were frequently filled with smoke at sufficient levels of concentration to cause noticeable irritation to the eyes. In the traditional open lean-tos people simply keep getting up and changing position frequently as the wind direction shifts but in the small closed houses of the resettlement the whole room can become filled with clouds of acrid smoke, particularly when damp wood is being burned in the several fires that smolder throughout the day. Burning of accumulated trash near the house sites produces a particularly acrid smoke. Suprisingly, no cases of serious eye inflammation were observed among the Semang.

Probably the major source of exposure to toxic gases comes from the practice of cigarette smoking which is heavily engaged in by Semang of both sexes and all ages from small children to the very elderly. Virtually anytime that Semang are not in actual physical motion they will be seen smoking with the relative scarcity of tobacco the only limiting factor on consumption rates. The need to obtain cash to purchase tobacco from the neighboring Malay *kampungs* is one of the strongest motivations for them to engage in production beyond their own minimal consumption needs.

The preferred cigarette is hand-rolled in a dry leaf using a very strong Malaysian-grown tobacco of the "Asli" brand. Manufactured cigarettes are occasionally smoked (especially when given as gifts by visiting anthropologists) but are considered of inferior flavor. Only one pipe was in use. Cigarettes are invariably smoked down to a minuscule butt, thus increasing the transmission of tar and nicotine to the smoker's lungs. In Western countries, heavy smoking, with consequent ingestion of tars and nicotine, has been correlated with increased incidence of lung cancer but no data on cancer incidence among the Semang are available. Respiratory diseases, especially tuberculosis, are quite common, however (personal communication from Nursing Sister Shirley Barnes, CUSO Volunteer attached to the JOA), and the incidence of such diseases may be related to heavy smoking.

Breathing of carbon monoxide carried in cigarette smoke also produces carboxyhemoglobin which interferes with the transport of oxygen by the blood. If the level of CO is high enough death can result as happens when running a car motor in a closed garage. As Mellanby (1972:19) points out, however, "higher levels of carbon monoxide are found in the blood of a smoker than in those exposed to the highest intensity of traffic fumes." In persons suffering from anemia, as is common among many Orang Asli, appreciable symptoms of oxygen deficiency might result, although no measurements of this were made.

Reference has already been made to the high levels of smoke observed in Semang shelters resulting from the small household fires that are kept burning around the clock. Smoke consists of fine carbon particles that are carried upward on the hot gases produced by the combustion of wood or other flammable substances. The thatch roofs of the more permanent Semang houses are blackened by the deposit of these particles although the traditional forest lean-tos are occupied for such short periods before abandonment that there is insufficient time for such airborne deposits to accumulate. From the Semang point of view the smoke is useful in that it tends to keep mosquitoes away from their dwellings. Given the physical discomfort caused by mosquito bites and the very real dangers of malarial infection, the long-term risks of air pollution would appear to be a secondary concern.

Burning of swidden fields is a major source of particulate matter to the atmosphere. If the felled trees and brush in the clearing are very dry when burned, an extremely intense fire results. A column of heated air rises thousands of meters above the earth's surface carrying along with it masses of carbon particles. The burning of swidden fields in the tropics as a whole may be responsible for a considerable magnitude of regional, and perhaps even global level air pollution (Root 1976). In northern Thailand, for example, Walker (1976:147) notes that, "in early April the burning of the swiddens fills the mountain air with fine ash particles which, in the absence of rain, seriously reduce visibility." I have observed similar effects from swidden burning in Sumatra. The area cleared by the Semang each year is so small, however, that their burning probably produces no more than a short-term and very localized impact on atmospheric air particle levels.

Soil blown into the air by wind also adds to the load of particles suspended in the atmosphere. The settlement at Sungai Rual is built on alluvial sandy soil and whenever several days pass without rain the paths and cleared spaces around the houses become quite dusty so that even a light breeze stirs up considerable dust clouds. Dust levels were measured using air particle traps constructed by placing a funnel with a 100 cm^2 mouth on top of a collection bottle partially filled with distilled water. One trap was placed in the settlement and a second about one kilometer away inside the undisturbed forest. After 22 days the contents were run through fiberglass filter papers which were then oven dried and weighed. The sediment trapped in the settlement weighed .082 grams compared to .038

grams in the forest. This can be extrapolated to an annual atmospheric particle deposition rate of 635 grams per square meter in the forest and 1,354 grams per square meter in the settlement.

Noxious Odors

The Semang do not pollute the atmosphere to any perceptible degree with unpleasant odors. Semang bathe frequently so that body odor is rarely noticeable even when several people are crowded together in one small shelter. Metabolic wastes are disposed of in the river so that no foci of decomposition are created within the settlement. Trash and debris from food preparation, cooking, and other activities are allowed to accumulate near and even inside the houses and this rubbish does often have an unpleasant odor but it is generally of a low intensity. Only during *kerdas* season, when large numbers of empty shells of this seed are dropped around the shelters, is there a strong smell present but this is not particularly unpleasant.

Disease Germs

Disease germs can be introduced into the atmosphere either directly through respiratory processes or secondarily through being blown from the ground into the air in association with particulate matter. The simple act of breathing disseminates many disease germs while sneezing and coughing blast astronomical numbers of germs into the surrounding atmosphere. As the Semang have no cultural prescription for covering of the mouth with the hand when coughing or sneezing, wide contamination of the surrounding air by sick individuals is permitted. Spitting and blowing of mucus on tracks, cleared areas around houses and even on the floor of shelters were frequently observed and can be a source of airborne disease germs when the infected soil is disturbed and contaminated dust blown into the air. Such pollution probably does not extend much beyond the community level although no measurement of the dispersal of airborne disease germs was attempted.

Electromagnetic and Sonic Pollution

Disturbance of sound, light and radio waves in the ecosystem can also be considered atmospheric pollution. Modern technology has, of course, produced massive pollution at a wide range of wave lengths. Thus, when the astronomer Carl Sagan was criticized for attaching a map showing earth's location onto an outward bound spacecraft for fear that it might reveal our position to hostile beings, he responded that it would be much simpler for them to just home in on the beacon provided by radio and television transmissions. Obviously, primitive people lack the technological capability to contribute to such pollution of the radio wave lengths, but the Semang do create a certain amount of disturbance of light and sound waves in the atmosphere.

Noise levels in the Semang settlement are generally quite low although, unfortunately, equipment for measuring decibel levels was unavailable. The people, however, are generally soft-spoken. Shouting, even among the children at play, is relatively uncommon, being restrained by strong religious taboos. Their economic activities also contribute relatively little noise to the environment with felling of trees and chopping of firewood perhaps creating the most noise. Discharge of shotguns by hunters is the activity producing sound at the highest decibel level but this is a rare event occurring no more than five or six times per month. The recent introduction of transistor radios is another nontraditional noise source. These radios are carried everywhere their owners go, usually playing at top volume, but, fortunately, the batteries soon run down and are only rarely replaced.

Night-time illumination is provided by fires, kerosene lanterns, and flashlights. These definitely add light rays into the night-time environment although certainly at such a low level of intensity as to only be perceptible within the immediate community.

Noise and light pollution produced by the Semang, although at low levels compared to modern societies, do have environmental implications in that they warn game animals of the presence of humans in the forest causing the animals to move out of the area, thus making the hunter's task more difficult.

Climate

Until recent years, when scientists became concerned with rising levels of carbon dioxide in the atmosphere due to growing use of fossil fuels, it had been assumed that human activity was unlikely to result in climatic modification. As recently as 1945 the geographer Huntington could write that

> ...nothing that man can yet do has any appreciable effect upon the weather, with its changes from day to day and season to season, or upon the climate with its variations in temperature, humidity, and wind. On the other hand, everyone knows that human feelings, health, and activity are extremely sensitive to weather and climate. [1959:257]

The relationship between humans and climate was thus seen as essentially undirectional with humans responding to meteorological factors without being able to influence them in turn. It is now known, of course, that human activities in the industrialized countries do, in fact, exert considerable influence over climate both at the local level, as in the case of the development of "heat islands" around major urban centers, and at the global level, as in the apparent long-term rise in atmospheric temperature due to the greenhouse effect associated with increasing levels of carbon dioxide concentration. What is surprising, however, is the extent to which even a low energy society, such as that of the Semang, can induce at least localized climatic changes.

The microclimate surrounding the body of the individual Semang is considerably modified by a number of their cultural practices. Air temperature, for example, is regulated by the wearing of clothing. Traditionally, the Semang have worn a minimum of clothing with men wearing only a narrow barkcloth loin cloth and women a very short skirt of rhizomes. Such clothing allows free circulation of air next to the skin with consequent rapid evaporation of perspiration and dissipation of body heat. In recent years, however, Semang men have adopted cotton shirts and trousers or sarongs while the women now always wear sarongs, and many wear brassieres and blouses as well. Such elaborate dress is generally worn, however, only in the settlement area and men hunting in the forest wear only shorts while women wear only a sarong. In the evening and the morning, when the moist air feels chill, people often wear an extra sarong pulled over their shoulders as sort of a cape or blanket. This retains a volume of still air close to the body as insulation against the cold. I can attest to the subjective difference this practice makes in one's sense of comfort.

No special protective clothing is used against rain but Semang have been observed to hold wild banana leaves over their heads thereby protecting their skin from the direct impact of the often rather cold drops. In comparison, use of rubberized ponchos or raincoats is quite impractical in the forest both because of the tendency of these materials to catch on branches and, more importantly, because the entrapment of perspiration under them caused one to rapidly become as wet as if one were directly exposed to the rain itself.

Traditional Semang housing is an open-fronted thatch-roofed lean-to. Inside is a bed-sitting platform made of split bamboo raised some 10 centimeters above ground level. This simple shelter both provides protection from the frequent jungle rains and damp mists and breaks the wind that accompanies storms. A fire burns continuously inside each shelter raising the air temperature and, perhaps more significantly in terms of perceived comfort, lowering the relative humidity. Unfortunately, the Semang fear of scientific instruments precluded the taking of measurements of wind speed, temperature and humidity inside their shelters to empirically verify my subjective impressions of these effects on the microclimate.

The clearance of an estimated 25 hectares of swidden fields at the Sungai Rual resettlement site has resulted in major changes in a number of climatic variables at the community level. It is unlikely that nomadic Semang traditionally cleared plots on such a scale but fields of this size are well within the range of forest-felling by neighboring swiddening groups such as the Temiar and the Semai. The Semang have also engaged in sporadic small-scale land clearance for agricultural purposes for as long as historical records are available so that such cleared areas are hardly to be ignored as being "modern" innovations.

To assess the climatic implications of such clearings, measurements of air temperature, soil and river water temperature, relative humidity, and precipitation were taken at two locations: one site in the center of the settlement and the other inside the primary forest approximately one kilometer from the settlement clearing. Both sites lay within the Sungai Rual valley at approximately the same elevation so that it can be reasonably assumed that any major differences in climatic readings taken at the same time at the two sites reflect human disturbance of the ecosystem.

Readings were taken on two days (17 and 19 April 1976) at two hour intervals. Because automatic recording equipment was not available, simultaneous readings were not possible as I had to make the measurements at one site and then walk to the other site where I repeated the readings half an hour later. Security considerations precluded going to the forest site after nightfall so that a full 24-hour cycle could not be observed. Any future study should use self-recording thermohydrographs rather than manual equipment to ensure simultaneous round the clock measurement of temperature and humidity.

Air Temperature

Air temperature was measured using a mercury thermometer held in the shade. Daytime air temperature was always higher in the settlement than in the forest, averaging 29.4° C in the settlement clearing compared to 27.2° C in the forest. There was a daily range of 11.3 degrees between the lowest and highest temperatures (22° to 33.3° C) in the settlement compared to 8.5 degrees (22° to 30.5° C) in the forest (Fig. 4a). Increased temperature levels

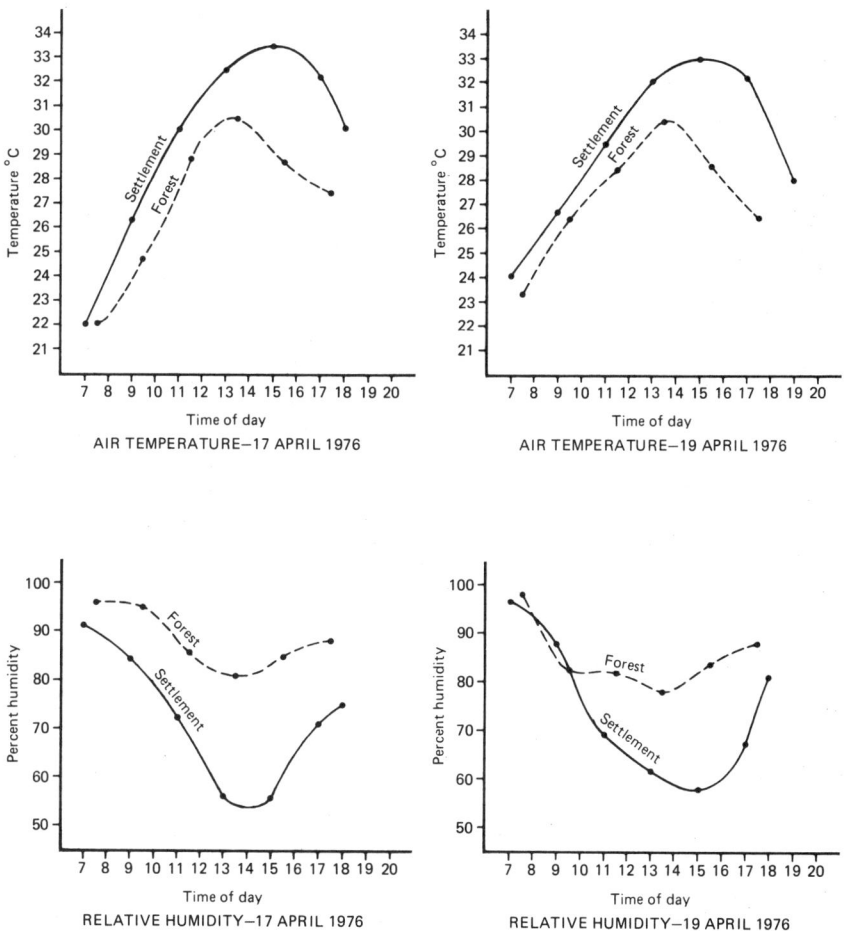

Figure 4. Comparison of air temperature and relative humidity in settlement and undisturbed forest.

in the settlement must be wholly attributed to its greater direct exposure to solar radiation, as the heat generated by the Semang population (metabolism, cooking fires, etc.) is clearly of insufficient magnitude to have a measurable effect on the air temperature beyond the household level.

Soil Temperature

Soil temperature was measured by inserting a mercury thermometer into the soil to a depth of 3 centimeters. The settlement measurement point was

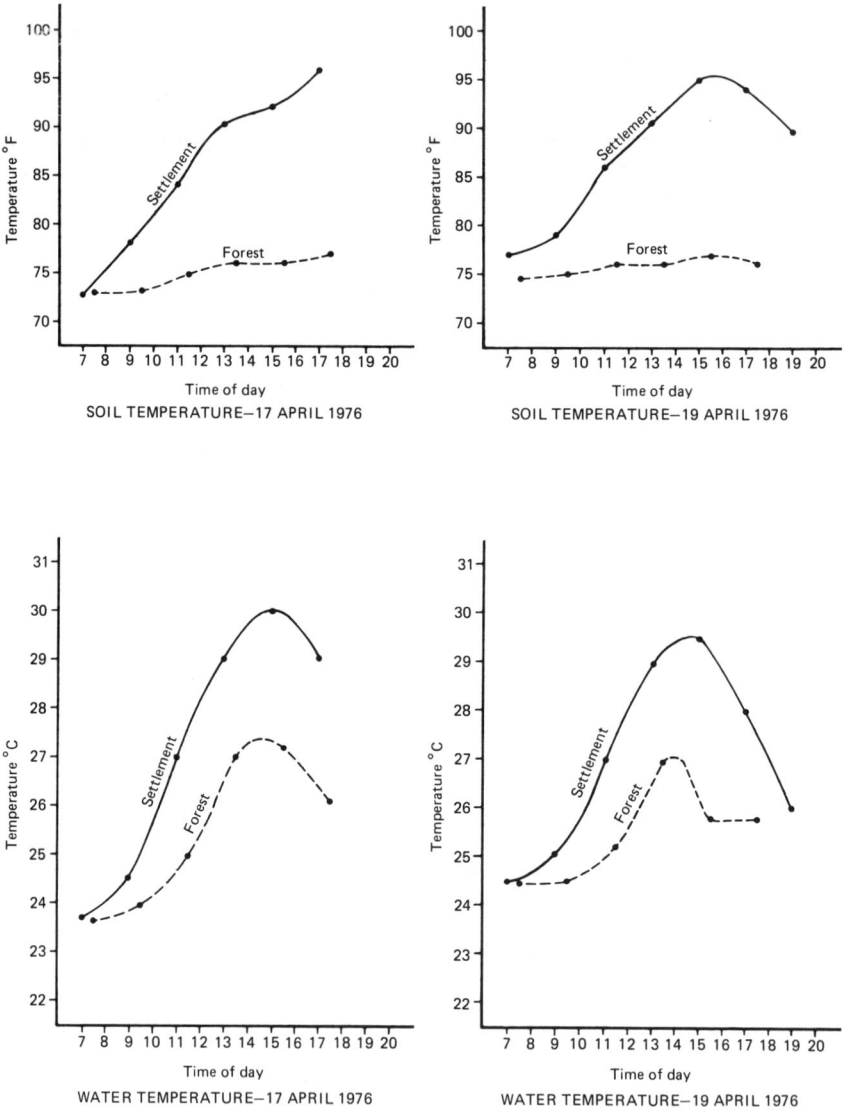

Figure 5. Comparison of soil and water temperature in settlement and undisturbed forest.

exposed to full sun throughout the day whereas the forest site was shaded by the overhead tree cover. Average soil temperature was 6° C higher in the settlement (30.1° C) than in the forest (24.1° C). The daily range from lowest to highest temperature shows an even greater disparity between the two locations than does air temperature with a range of 13.1 degrees between the lowest (22.5° C) and highest (35.6° C) soil temperature measured in the settlement compared to a range of only 2.2 degrees between the lowest (22.8° C) and the highest (25° C) temperature recorded in the forest soil (Fig. 5a).

Water Temperature

Temperature of water in the Rual River was taken at a point where it had flowed exposed to the direct sunlight through the settlement clearing for some 200 meters. Water temperature was also taken in a small tributary stream flowing in the forest near where the other forest climatic data were collected. A mercury thermometer was held in the flowing water to a depth of 10 centimeters for 30 seconds to obtain the water temperature reading. Water temperatures in the two locations followed a similar trend to that displayed by air and soil temperatures (Fig. 5b) with the water in the settlement warming sooner and achieving higher temperatures in the course of the day than the water in the forest stream. The average daytime temperature for the forest stream water was 25.5° C while that of the river in the settlement was 27.1° C, a difference of 1.6 degrees. The river water in the settlement showed a maximum daily range of 6.3 degrees (23.7° to 30° C) whereas the stream in the forest varied by only 3.5 degrees (23.7° to 27.2° C). Such increased temperature levels and greater range of variation may have considerable effect on the aquatic life supported in the river although no study was made of this ecosystem component.

Relative Humidity

Relative humidity levels were measured using a Cassela sling hygrometer. Average daytime relative humidity was much higher in the forest (86.8%) than in the settlement clearing (73.2%) but the daily range of variation in humidity was greatest in the settlement site. There, relative humidity varied from a low reading of 55.5% at 1300 hours to a high of 96% at 0700 hours while in the forest 78.5% was the lowest recorded level with 96% the highest (Fig. 4b).

Air Movement

No equipment for recording wind speed was available but I observed that, except during severe storms, there was rarely any perceptible motion of air in the forest whereas there was generally a breeze estimated at 2 to 10 kilometers per hour blowing in the settlement clearing. This made a very noticeable difference in perceived comfort level, with the cooling produced by the air movement more than offsetting the higher air temperature in the open area. In contrast, the still air and high relative humidity within the forest resulted in a sense of oppressive heat even though the air temperature was considerably lower than in the settlement.

Precipitation

Rainfall was measured using cans with 5 inch diameter mouths placed on the ground surface. There was measurable rainfall on 14 out of 22 days in the forest and 15 out of 22 days in the settlement. A greater total volume of precipitation was also recorded in the settlement (188 mm) than in the forest (156 mm) with volume of fall in the settlement exceeding that in the forest on 10 days while volume in the forest exceeded that in the settlement on only 5 days. I have no adequate explanation for these differences although it is probable that a proportion of the rain that hit the upper stories of the forest canopy was channeled to the ground along the tree trunks and thus was not recorded in the gauge. It may also be that the higher temperatures of soil and air at the settlement clearing caused marginally greater precipitation through heating of low-lying clouds.

Water

The quality of river water has been altered by the Semang in several ways: (1) increased sediment loads as a result of erosion due to disturbance of the soil by agriculture and other activities; (2) introduction of bacteria, protozoa and other parasitic organisms from the use of the river as a toilet; (3) increased nutrient levels from the use of laundry soap and detergent and introduction of feces and urine into water; (4) introduction of toxins from the use of derris root to poison fish.

Sediment Loads

Any disturbance of the forest soil increases its vulnerability to erosion with consequent increased runoff of suspended sediments and dissolved solids into the rivers. Shifting cultivation of the sort practiced by the Semang and other Malaysian Orang Asli groups is frequently blamed for being a major cause of soil erosion. It is undoubtedly the case that, where population density achieves sufficient levels to necessitate over-rapid recycling of swidden plots, breakdown of soil structure occurs with consequent increased sedimentation of the rivers. The Semang population is still very small, however, while the area available for cultivation is very large so that the swidden cycle has not yet been unduly compressed. Measurements of sediment loads in the Rual River after it has passed through the settled area show very low levels of suspended sediments and dissolved solids although the average weight of suspended sediments is slightly higher there than in water samples taken above the settlement in an undisturbed forest stream.

On seven occasions sets of water samples were taken in 500 ml bottles simultaneously at three sampling sites: a small tributary stream running through high forest and joining the main river about 200 meters above the settlement; the main river at a point about 250 meters upstream from the settlement; and the main river after it had flowed through most of the settled and cultivated area. Three sets of samples were taken on days with no rain when the river was relatively low and clear while four sets of samples were taken immediately following heavy rainfalls when the water level was high and turbidity pronounced. Water samples were subsequently analyzed by filtering out the suspended settlements onto Millipore filters which were then oven-dried and weighed. The weight of the sediment was determined by subtracting the weight of the filter after passing the water through it from its weight before use. The filtered water was then poured into pre-weighed crucibles and evaporated over a heated water bath in order to find the weight of dissolved solids. Finally, the crucible with its dissolved solids was placed in an oven and the carbon burned off in order to determine the organic content of the dissolved solids. No determination of carbon content of the suspended sediments was possible as the filtrate was of insufficient mass to survive firing.

As Table 1 shows, suspended sediment loads are generally quite low at all sampling sites regardless of the state of the river. The highest mean concentration (42.5 parts per million) and the highest concentration in a single sample (149 ppm) were recorded for water in the river after it had passed through the settlement and acquired surface runoff from the living and agricultural area. On three occasions, however, the water had a higher suspended sediment load above the settlement than below while in one test the forest stream water had a higher weight of sediments than did water drawn from either site in the main river. Such variation may in part reflect

TABLE 1
Suspended Sediment Levels (in Parts per Million)
in River Water Samples Taken at Rual Post

Date of sample	Stream in forest	Rual River above Semang settlement	Rual River below Semang settlement	State of river
21 April 1976	0.6	1.6	2.2	low
22 April 1976	3.6	0.2	0.6	low
25 April 1976	9.0	13.6	149.0	high
26 April 1976	7.6	10.8	8.8	medium
28 April 1976	50.0	1.0	26.0	low
5 May 1976	80.2	141.8	105.2	very high
6 May 1976	4.2	7.8	5.4	medium
Average level	22.2	25.3	42.5	-

variation in intensity of rainfall in different parts of the watershed on different days.

Dissolved solids were present in low concentrations in water samples taken from all three sites with only slight average differences between the three series (Table 2). The river water below the settlement had a slightly higher mean dissolved solid level (44.2 ppm) compared to 42 ppm for the river above the settlement and 43.1 ppm in the forest stream. Dissolved solids concentrations were higher in water samples from below the settlement than in the water taken from above the settlement in six out of seven comparisons. The forest stream water had higher levels of dissolved solids concentrations than either river site in three out of seven samples.

TABLE 2
Dissolved Solids Levels (in Parts per Million)
in Water Samples Taken at Rual Post

Date of sample	Stream in forest	Rual River above Semang settlement	Rual River below Semang settlement	State of river
21 April 1976	46.2	41.6	44.6	low
22 April 1976	49.6	45.6	47.6	low
25 April 1976	39.2	36.0	39.2	high
26 April 1976	48.6	49.8	50.0	medium
28 April 1976	39.0	43.0	42.8	low
5 May 1976	42.2	36.6	39.6	very high
6 May 1976	37.2	41.2	45.6	medium
Average level	43.1	42.0	44.2	-

The forest stream had the highest average organic content in its dissolved solids (35.7%) compared to 32.3% for the river above the settlement and 33.9% for the river after passing through the settlement (Table 3). The forest stream had the highest percentage of organic contents in four out of seven sample comparisons.

TABLE 3
Organic Component as Percentage of Total Dissolved Solids in River Water Samples Taken at Rual Post

Date of sample	Stream in forest	Rual River above Semang settlement	Rual River below Semang settlement	State of river
21 April 1976	36.4	31.7	33.2	low
22 April 1976	34.3	29.8	31.5	low
25 April 1976	36.2	27.2	37.2	high
26 April 1976	32.1	33.3	34.4	medium
28 April 1976	33.3	29.8	29.9	low
5 May 1976	44.1	36.6	36.4	very high
6 May 1976	33.9	37.4	35.1	medium
Mean percentage	35.7%	32.3%	33.9%	-

Semang activity, particularly clearing of land for agriculture and house sites, does therefore appear to somewhat increase suspended sediment loads in the river water and this increased loading may affect the quality of river water well beyond the bounds of the local ecosystem. The magnitude of change is small, however, in comparison to sediment levels resulting from modern logging, agricultural and construction activity. Samples of water from the Langat River in Selangor, taken by students for a twenty day period, show average suspended sediment levels of 6.2 ppm in the forested headwaters near a Temuan aboriginal settlement, 18.5 ppm in an old established Malay *kampung* a few kilometers downstream, and 1,228 ppm near the limit of tidal influence after the river has passed through an area of tin mines and plantation agriculture.

Disease Organisms

Use of rivers as toilets can introduce a wide variety of disease organisms into the water. These organisms may then infect downstream populations who drink or bathe in the contaminated water. Bacteria, amoebas, and various parasitic worms can all be transmitted by contaminated water. Like many other indigenous Southeast Asian populations, the Semang defecate directly into the river and then cleanse themselves with river water which flows back into the stream. Given the presence of several infectious diseases and parasites among the Semang, some contamination of downstream water must occur. In view of the small size of the Semang population and the high velocity with which water flows in the Rual River, such contamination is probably pulsating rather than continuous.

Three water samples taken from the forest stream and three samples from the river below the settlement were subjected to the "Hach test" for presence of fecal bacteria. Two samples from each site developed gas bubbles in the presumptive test bottles. All four samples were positive for presence of fecal bacteria after transferral to confirmation testing bottles. The water is thus definitely contaminated with fecal bacteria although the method of testing is not able to discriminate between bacteria of human and other animal origins. It is possible that the water in the forest stream is carrying bacteria from the feces of wild forest mammals that would not represent any health threat to the Semang population.

Nutrients

Many human activities add nutrients into water supplies often resulting in the eutrophication of restricted bodies, such as lakes. The Semang do add some small quantities of organic materials and chemical nutrients to the water in the form of feces and soap residues, which may serve as food for fish. Analysis with Hach test kits of two water samples from the forest stream and the river running through the settlement did not detect the presence of nitrate, ammonia, or phosphate at measurable levels and, given the relatively great flow rate of the Rual River and the small size of the Semang population, it is unlikely that the Semang produce any significant change in nutrient levels in the downstream waters, although their inputs may be important for local fish populations.

Derris Root Poisoning of Fish

Throughout Southeast Asia, indigenous populations add the sap of the derris root *(tuba)* to the waters of streams and rivers in an effort to poison the fish there. Derris breaks down rapidly and does not pose a a long-term threat to riverine life, but the poison in the derris sap causes paralysis in fish, even at very low concentrations, and they float to the surface where they can easily be caught by hand. The method can be a highly productive technique from the human point of view but since it is nonselective, killing small fish as well as large ones, and since its effects may be felt far downstream from where it is actually applied, it has very disruptive impact on riverine fish populations. Its use has been legally banned in Malaysia for many years but limited covert use continues, especially among more isolated Orang Asli groups. The Semang formerly engaged in this practice but no use of *tuba* was made during my stay at Sungai Rual, in part because the fish remaining in the river are too small and few in number to make the exercise worthwhile. According to Alberto Gomes (personal communication) chemical insecticide purchased in Jeli was used to poison fish in the river in early 1979. If such usage becomes common it could have unfortunate consequences for populations living downstream.

Other Effects on the Water

The Semang withdraw water from the river and carry it in bamboo tubes to their shelters where it is kept for use in cooking and for drinking. The quantity involved hardly exceeds 10 liters per day per household so has no significant effect on downstream water supply. The channeling of springs into bamboo pipelines for domestic use (a practice common to other Orang Asli groups as well) may affect the plant and animal communities in the immediate area of the spring but such impact is on a microscale compared to the total rain forest area. Other activities such as walking in the streams when fishing or traveling cross country may stir up sediments and shift rocks causing temporary change in water quality and flow rates but again always on a very minor scale.

In conclusion, it can be said that the Semang have relatively little measurable impact on water quality. Their forest clearance for settlement and agricultural purposes produces only slight increases in sediment loads while use of the river for toilet and laundry purposes makes only minor additions to the available nutrient supplies in the local area. Introduction of human disease organisms and substances poisonous to fish life are the most serious and far reaching consequences of Semang interaction with the river system.

The Soil

Human activities affect soil by (1) changing nutrient levels, (2) disturbing structure and causing surface erosion, (3) adding waste materials, (4) polluting it with disease organisms and (5) consuming substrate materials. The Semang affect the soil component of their ecosystem in all of these ways, although change of nutrient levels, erosion and pollution with disease organisms are the most important effects.

Changes in Nutrient Levels

The quantity and concentration of nutrient elements, particularly nitrogen, phosphorus, and potassium in the soil may be considerably modified by human actions. Clearing of forest cover may accelerate nutrient loss to leaching and soil erosion, a problem that will be discussed under erosion in general. Burning of swidden fields destroys much organic nitrogen but releases quantities of other nutrients stored in the biomass back into the soil, temporarily increasing the fertility of the field. Such nutrients are either quickly absorbed by the crop plants or are washed away by the heavy rainfall into the river system and hence are exported out of the local ecosystem. Planting of legumes such as groundnuts and long beans in the swiddens may restore some nitrogen to the soil but the Semang do not grow sufficiently large quantities of either crop to have much positive effect, while their main food plants of manioc and maize are notoriously heavy consumers of nutrients.

The Semang may also contribute to considerable fertility migration within their ecosystem: Crops and wild foodstuffs produced over a wide area are collected and are processed and consumed within the small settlement area. Nutrients in foodstuffs consumed by the Semang are not recycled into the terrestrial ecosystem because their custom of using the river for toilet purposes causes nutrients contained in metabolites to be carried downstream out of the local system. Nutrients contained in waste products from processing of forest produce, such as the pods of *kerdas,* collect around the settlement area where they are either burned or allowed to decompose with consequent increase in levels of nutrients in the settlement site soil. Unfortunately, soil samples taken for this study were lost while being processed in the laboratory of the Faculty of Agriculture but it is known from studies in Indochina that very considerable concentrations of phosphorus can be built up around areas of human settlement and that these high levels can persist for many years after abandonment of the site (Castagnol 1939).

A more significant aspect of fertility migration may be the export from the forest to the urban areas of Malaysia and abroad of quantities of organic materials. The Semang, like most Malaysian aborigines, are heavily engaged in collection of wild forest products such as rattan, *petai,* and *kerdas,* durian and other fruit, medicinal plants, monkeys and other jungle animals, etc. These components of the forest ecosystem biomass are exported for sale in the neighboring Malay villages and ultimately to the cities and foreign markets. In return the Semang purchase rice, salt, sugar, dried fish, tinned sardines, parangs, sarongs, matches, kerosene, and luxury goods such as mirrors, soap, cosmetics, flashlights, transistor radios, etc. The flow of nutrients through the system appears to be highly asymmetrical with the forest suffering a continual deficit. In any one year the total quantity of nutrients lost may be relatively small but when it is considered that this trade pattern has existed for hundreds and probably thousands of years (Dunn 1975) the cumulative loss suffered by the forest ecosystem may be quite major. The loss is especially important given the very low nutrient levels in most Malaysian forest soils.

Disturbance of Soil Structure and Surface Erosion

Surface erosion and disturbance of soil structure are usually linked effects of human activities. The Semang affect soil structure through their normal hunting and gathering activities which lead to creation of tracks in the forest having highly compacted soil. As these tracks generally run almost straight up and down hill slopes they form channels for runoff of heavy rainfalls and thus to some extent promote soil erosion. The total surface area covered by such tracks in the forest ecosystem is extremely small, however, and the consequent soil loss is relatively minor compared to the impact of even one bulldozed logging road.

Clearance of land for agriculture and settlement sites has a more significant impact on soil erosion rates. Exposure of forest soil to the direct sun leads to rapid loss of organic contents with consequent compaction of soil particles. Such soils are more vulnerable to erosion than those retaining a strong particulate structure. More important, the clearance of the overhead forest cover exposes the soil surface to the direct impact of the heavy tropical rains. The large, high velocity drops hit the surface with full force instead of having their kinetic energy dissipated by striking the leaves and branches of the canopy of the forest as is the case in the undisturbed ecosystem.

The effect of forest clearance on the striking impact of rain was measured by placing cups filled with pre-weighed quantities of sand in the settlement clearing and in the high forest. Each cup had a mesh bottom and was set in a pan of water so that the sand was kept moist and thus was not subject to being blown away by the wind. Following each rainstorm, the contents of the cups were oven dried and weighed and the new weights compared with the original weights to determine the percentage of sand lost due to being struck by the rain.

Five comparative tests were made with rate of soil loss greater in the

TABLE 4
Soil Loss Due to Rainfall Impact at Rual Post

FOREST AREA		SETTLEMENT CLEARED AREA	
Rainfall (inches)	Percent of soil lost from cup	Rainfall (inches)	Percent of soil lost from cup
.42	17.7	.33	16.9
.48	13.1	.40	22.1
1.14	18.1	1.21	30.1
.92	18.9	.99	26.0
.30	19.0	.26	22.6

clearing than in the forest in four trials (Table 4). Mean soil loss in the forest was 17.4% compared to 23.4% in the settlement clearing and total loss of soil due to rainfall impact was approximately 25 percent greater in the open than in the forest.

Deposition of Waste Materials

Human activities inevitably generate quantities of waste products which must somehow be disposed of. Burning, dumping into rivers, and dumping onto the soil surface are the primary means by which the Semang dispose of their refuse.

The Semang do not generate large quantities of wastes in contrast to the immense quantities produced by modern industrial societies. In the United States, for instance, each man, woman and child reportedly accounts for more than two kilograms of solid wastes per day (Southwick 1976: 62-63). Most of the Semang waste materials are organic ones such as pods from *petai* and *kerdas*, bones from game animals, leftover fragments of bamboo from blowpipe construction, etc., but there is a small but increasing quantity of inorganic refuse in the form of empty tin cans and bottles, burned-out batteries, and empty plastic bags.

The Semang have no cultural patterns favoring maintenance of cleanliness around their dwellings so that wastes are simply discarded on the spot. This posed little problem in their traditional nomadic life in the forest but has resulted in extensive concentration of refuse in the resettlement area where one site has been continuously occupied for several years. House floors are filthy. They are rarely or never swept. In one house the floor was covered by a layer of refuse between two and five centimeters deep composed of sand, ashes and charred wood from the several cooking fires, old banana leaves that had been used for wrapping food, empty sardine tins, plastic bags and cellophane wrappers, spilled rice, fish bones, pith from manioc spit out after chewing out the starch, bits of rotting banana, *kerdas* pods, flashlight batteries, empty soft drink bottles, etc.

On several occasions during the one month period of observation one or several women swept up refuse that was lying in the open area between the houses. This refuse was simply swept into piles a few meters away from the house sites where it was either burned or sometimes simply left to decay.

Pollution with Disease Organisms

The Semang may pollute the soil around their settlements with disease organisms through spitting and blowing of mucus onto the ground. People spit regardless of wherever they may be when they feel the need, including inside their houses. Chewing of betel increases the incidence of spitting which, in a population having carriers of tuberculosis, is a likely way of spreading infection. The Semang population is so small, however, that such practices probably presented no threat when living the traditional dispersed nomadic style of life in the forest, although given the greater density at the resettlement site, they may now pose some danger to public health.

Fecal pollution of soil is not a great problem given the common practice of using rivers for toilet purposes. Forest soil fauna such as ants and beetles were observed to consume feces deposited on the surface within twelve hours in any case.

Consumption of Substrate Materials

The Semang make almost no cultural usage of stone. These Malaysian nomads make no implements from stone and have not done so at any time within their known history. The only significant uses of stone at present are: (1) bits of quartzite are used as strike-a-lights for hitting against a piece of steel to make fires, (2) rounded pieces of basalt-like rock from the rivers are used to sharpen knives, (3) large river stones are used to support cooking pots in the fires, and (4) quartz crystals are employed by the shamans to cure disease (Rambo 1979a).

Unlike the Negritos of the Andaman Islands, the Semang make no pottery. Red ochre and white clays are used for painting designs on their faces, both for purposes of adornment and for ritual curing purposes. A type of whitish clay is also eaten as a remedy for stomach disturbances. Such uses of substrate materials are of such minor magnitude as to have no perceptible impact on supplies of these resources nor do they require significant disruption of the soil surface to obtain needed supplies.

Plants

The Semang exert impact on the floral component of their ecosystem in five ways: (1) clearing the forest for settlement sites, tracks, and swidden fields; (2) collecting wild plant materials such as fruit, rattan, and wood; (3) manipulating growing conditions of wild species; (4) disseminating seeds of wild species; and (5) introducing domesticated species into the forest ecosystem.

Forest Clearing

The Semang cut down any plant that interferes with desired human activities. When a new shelter is established in the forest, any shrubs and small trees within the circle of the lean-tos will be chopped down with parangs. Larger trees are generally not cut although if the camp is inhabited for a period exceeding a few days they too may be cut down.

When walking in the forest both men and women customarily carry bush knives in their hands and hack down any small vegetation that bars their chosen route. In general, however, the line of least resistance is followed so that larger trees are avoided and detours made around patches of extremely thick vegetation that develop where the fall of aged forest trees has exposed the ground to direct sunlight. Around the area of permanent settlement several tracks have been established leading to sites of frequently exploited resources and all users contribute to keeping these open by chopping or breaking off any creepers or branches that happen to block the way.

Relatively large areas are cleared and burned to open swidden fields for agricultural purposes. The *ladang* at Sungai Rual is about 25 hectares but this is the result of government encouragement. Traditional fields were much smaller, probably never exceeding one or two hectares in area and being opened only on a very sporadic basis. Such fields are usually cultivated for only a single season before being abandoned and the forest allowed to regenerate. Dense brush and creepers will cover the clearing within a single year but succession to mature forest exceeds fifty years.

Clearing of swidden fields is selective with wild fruit trees left standing. The giant *toalang* tree *(Koompassia excelsa),* which has extremely hard wood, is also left standing because, in the words of one Semang informant, "the axe can't eat it." This tree is a popular nesting site for wild honey bees, which may be another reason that the honey-loving Semang leave it uncut.

Collection of Forest Plant Products

Semang survival is dependent upon collection of wild forest plants both for their own consumption and for trade with outside markets to obtain cash to buy rice and other needed commodities. More time is spent on forest collecting than any other activity and a very wide range of plants and plant products is exploited. The principal products collected for sale during my visits to the Sungai Rual settlement were rattan, *petai (Parkia speciosa)* and *kerdas (Pithecellobium jiringa)*. Various other roots, herbs, and flowers are collected for medicinal use and especially for sale to Malays and Chinese who highly value Orang Asli medical plants, particularly those with reputed aphrodisiacal qualities. In earlier times, tree resins collectively called *damar* were gathered for use as torch fuel and for sale for making into varnish but introduction of kerosene lamps and battery-powered flashlights and decline of the world market for natural varnishes has brought a virtual halt to this activity. Collection of these products is generally done with little concern for possible damage to the plants. For example, Semang were observed to cut entire branches from *kerdas* trees when gathering the edible seed pods.

Cultivated plants are harvested in the same casual manner as in the case of wild species. Semang women were observed on several occasions harvesting chili peppers growing in their *ladang* by breaking off whole sections of stem, leaves and fruit together. These branches were then carried back to the shelters where the fruits were later separated from the unwanted plant material.

Wild yams, particularly *ubi garam*, are collected as the staple wild starch although cultivated manioc and purchased rice are much preferred. The wild tubers are dug out from the soil with a digging stick. Contrary to reported conservation practices among other aboriginal groups who are said to rebury a piece of tuber to assure regeneration of the plant, the Semang appear to take away all parts found.

Bamboos of several species are used for construction of houses and other artifacts. Water is carried and stored in sections of green bamboo 5 to 10 centimeters in diameter and 1 meter to 1.5 meters in length. Traditionally such large bamboo sections were also used for cooking as water will boil in the green tubes before the fire dries them sufficiently to burn. Metal cooking pots are increasingly displacing bamboo, however, although all Semang still know of this use and continue to cook in bamboo on occasion. Large bamboo is cut freely and any parts that do not meet the standards of the collector or are surplus to immediate needs are simply left where they fall as the supply is seen as unlimited, a not overly optimistic judgment given the speed with which bamboo grows.

One species *(Bambusa wrayi)* has particularly long internodes and is thus suitable for making unjointed blowpipes. Only a few groves exist in the Main Range and each is reportedly controlled by a particular aboriginal community (Noone 1955). The Semang at Sungai Rual know of one grove on the Perak-Kelantan border and whenever they need new blowpipes make the long trek there. They say that any member of the band is entitled to cut whatever amount he desires and the principal safeguard against over-exploitation appears to be the remoteness of the grove.

Fires are kept smoldering round the clock in Semang shelters so that a considerable quantity of wood is burned as fuel. Dead fallen trees in the forest and unburned trunks and branches from the swiddens are collected for firewood. Despite high consumption there appears to be no shortage of suitable wood in the immediate vicinity of the settlement.

Manipulation of Growing Conditions of Wild Plants

Many primitive "preagricultural" peoples actively manipulate natural ecosystems so as to increase their productivity. The Semang are no exception since they deliberately burn bamboo clumps in the forest, both, according to the statements of informants, to clear them of accumulated litter making it easier to get at the stalks, and because burning promotes growth of new shoots. Larger scale manipulation of the tropical rainforest by burning is of course precluded by its general dampness, so that the impact of the Semang on the successional dynamics of the forest remains minimal.

Dissemination of Wild Species in the Forest

The Semang may help to distribute seeds of various wild plant species over wide areas of the forest. Wild fruits such as durian are often taken from the parent trees and carried back to the shelter site for later consumption there and it is possible that some of the discarded seeds may generate in the new location. Abandoned camps would provide especially suitable places for seedlings to get started as the underbrush has been cleared away thus reducing initial competition for light and nutrients, and there may also be some residual enrichment of the soil by nutrients contained in the ashes of the cooking fires and the debris discarded by the Semang. No observations of such seed generation were made, however, and this impact can only be advanced as a plausible hypothesis. There is no evidence that the Semang deliberately plant seeds of wild species that they desire to propagate although, as noted above, they do take measures to encourage the growth of already established wild plants. For example, wild durian groves are reportedly kept clear of bushes that might compete with this highly valued source of fruit.

Introduction of Domesticated Species

Plants cultivated in the Semang swiddens are in most cases domesticates that are not found in the forest under natural conditions. Many of these species (maize, manioc, papaya, chili peppers, sweet potatoes, peanuts) are alien introductions from the New World. Such cultigens, and the weed species that accompany them, form an unstable association that can only be maintained in the tropical forest through continuous human intervention. Swiddens abandoned for even one year begin to be reclaimed by wild species. The only cultigens that appear to persist for any time are the papaya, pineapple, and the banana, although even these will eventually be shaded out by the regenerating forest. While still in early successional stages, however, the swidden plots form an important food resource for many wild animal species.

Animals

The Semang affect the faunal component of their ecosystem through (1) predation by hunting and fishing, (2) creation of new niches and alteration of existing ones, and (3) introduction of new species.

Predation

Semang hunting and fishing appear to have considerable impact on the faunal populations of their ecosystem. The traditional bow and arrow was effective for killing large game such as rhinoceros, tapir, deer, and wild pig, while the muskets and, later, shotguns which replaced bows and arrows in colonial times are even more efficient killers of large game. I have argued elsewhere (Rambo 1978) that aboriginal hunting using firearms has profoundly affected the populations of large mammals in the Malayan rain forest. In the one month period of observation for this study Semang hunters killed two barking deer and four wild pigs.

The Semang concentrate their efforts on the hunting of small game such as squirrels and monkeys which can be killed with poisoned blowpipe darts rather than scarce and expensive shotgun shells. Men often but not always carry their blowpipes with them on trips into the forest to collect plant products and will take any opportunity to shoot an animal that arises but on the whole they are not avid hunters and rarely make special hunting trips. Their shooting ability is not as highly developed as one would expect and they were observed to miss a number of relatively easy shots, both with blowpipes and shotguns. It is difficult to evaluate the effect of Semang hunting on small mammals. Successful hunters are secretive about their catch to avoid having to share it with others so that it was impossible to obtain any record of the number of animals killed during the field work. It was my impression that only a few squirrels and other small mammals were taken, however.

Trapping of animals, although a major means of meat procurement among neighboring Senoi groups such as the Temiar, is rarely done by the Semang although all males say that they know how to make traps.

Fish are caught using throw nets (purchased from neighboring Malays), derris root poison, woven bamboo traps, and by "tickling" under rocks with their hands. Recently, goggles and rubberband-powered spear guns have been adopted from the Malays. Most of the larger fish in the Sungai Rual have been caught and only ones under 10 centimeters in length are still common. Nevertheless, the Semang still spend considerable time in fishing and continue to derive a considerable share of their protein supply from this source although they complain about declining yields. Some blame the lessened fish population on Malays and Chinese whom they accuse of using dynamite in parts of the river but others recognize that the relatively dense Semang population in the resettlement area has overfished the local streams.

Small wild animals such as monkeys and bamboo rats are occasionally captured as infants and are raised in capitivity as pets. One bamboo rat was being raised in this fashion during the period of field work. Monkeys may be sold to the Malays for use in gathering coconuts.

Habitat Changes

Alteration of the environment as an indirect consequence of human activities probably has greater effect on most faunal populations than does direct predation. Humans both destroy existing niches, as when the forest is cleared, and create new ones, as when settlements are built. In the process, some species lose and others gain but all are affected somehow.

In the deep forest the Semang are probably most important as a source of food to other organisms. The people are greatly afraid of tigers and at least one adult Semang was killed by a tiger within the memory of living Semang. Tigers are still common in the area of Sungai Rual and a very large one was seen several times only one kilometer from the settlement while we were there. A band living in lean-tos in the forest will abandon its camping site and move some distance away if a tiger is believed to be in the neighborhood. More significant, however, in terms of actual frequency of feeding, are smaller organisms, particularly leeches and mosquitoes.

The forest in the Sungai Rual area abounds with leeches and even the vigilant Semang, who wear few clothes and are quick to observe and brush off any leeches that crawl onto them, are frequently bitten (although not nearly as frequently as are people who wear long trousers and boots which conceal the presence of these parasites until after they have become attached). Surprisingly, there is a religious taboo on killing leeches and those that are detected are simply brushed off. To burn a leech or slice it with a parang is believed to bring down the wrath of *Karei*.

Mosquitoes of various species, some of them vectors for malaria, are abundant in parts of the forest although they are almost absent from the resettlement area. The Semang supply food to the mosquitoes and also on occasion become infected with the malarial protozoa carried by the *Anopheles* species. Recent disruption of the forest around Sungai Rual by extensive logging operations may have increased the incidence of infection. Other than sleeping next to smokey fires, they have no defense against mosquitoes although they may have some genetic defense against malaria in the form of abnormal hemoglobin E. Unfortunately, no Semang populations have been tested for this blood type although high incidences are recorded for the Senoi (Lie-Injo et al. 1972).

The Semang are afflicted by a wide variety of internal parasites (Dunn 1972). No statistical data on levels of infection among the people at Sungai Rual are available but many of the children have distended stomachs which Department of Aboriginal Affairs medical personnel attribute to these parasites.

The Semang customarily bury their dead in a grave dug in the forest soil where the corpse would represent a source of energy and nutrients to decomposer organisms. The small size of the Semang population would make this a relatively minor contribution to the bioenergetics of the total forest ecosystem. Semang use of the river for purposes of defecation may, however, represent a more substantial nutritional input to the aquatic fauna in the waters downstream from their settlements.

Clearance of the forest for farming and settlement sites radically modifies the environment. It changes a complex system into a very simplified one. The high net productivity of swiddens, both while still actively cultivated and in the first few years after abandonment, provides plentiful food for herbivorous animals. Wild pigs and barking deer are particularly attracted to the foraging offered by the swidden sites. In fact, the only deer I observed in the period spent studying the Semang were grazing at dusk in a small swidden that had been abandoned about one year earlier. Predators, particularly hawks, are also attracted to the Semang swiddens by the proliferation of small rodents there. One or more hawks of undetermined species could be observed almost every day perching on a large dead tree on a slope commanding a good view of most of the *ladang*.

Bird life is generally impoverished in the swiddens compared to the undisturbed forest. Only eight species were resident in the settlement site and *ladang* at Rual Post: greater coucal, giant spinetail swift, house swift, common brown babbler, yellow-vented bulbul, magpie robin, wren warbler, and white-rumped munia. Seven other species were occasional visitors (Table 5). All are species known for their association with areas disturbed by human activity. In contrast, Dunn (1975:56) reports observing about 130 species of birds in an undisturbed forest area in Ulu Selangor.

TABLE 5
Birds Observed in the Settlement Area at Sungai Rual
(9 – 17 April 1978)

Common name	Scientific name	Number present	Number of days observed
House swift	*Apus affinis*	20+	8
Giant spinetail swift	*Chaetura gigantea*	5–10	8
Magpie robin	*Copsychus gaularis*	2–4	8
White-rumped munia	*Lonchura striata*	5–20	8
Wren warbler	*Prinia* (spec.)	1–4	4
Greater coucal	*Centropus sinensis*	1	4
Common brown babbler	*Malacocincla abbotti*	1	3
Yellow-vented bulbul	*Pycnonotus goiavier*	2	2
Crested serpent eagle	*Spilornis cheela*	1	2
White-breasted kingfisher	*Halcyon smyrnensis*	1	2
Swallow	*Hirundo* (spec.)	20+	1
Common tailor bird	*Orthotomus sutorius*	2	1
Spider hunter	*Arachnothera* (spec.)	2	1
Bronzed drongo	*Dicrurus aeneus*	1	1
Richard's pipit	*Anthus movaeseelandiae*	1	1

The primary faunal beneficiaries of Semang habitat modification appear to be the insects, particularly cockroaches and houseflies. Neither organism is found in the unmodified forest but both are present in relatively great numbers in the settlement site. Cockroaches, in particular, thrive in the rich organic litter on the floors of the Semang houses. Sitting in any of the older houses is quite an unpleasant experience as one must constantly brush cockroaches off one's body. A main motive for building of new houses is to temporarily escape the infestation of roaches, few of which are found in the temporary lean-tos in the forest.

Houseflies are present in the settlement site in considerable numbers and a few were also observed in one of the shelters in the forest, although none are present in the undisturbed forest itself. A fly trap baited with bread, brown sugar, and vinegar, based on the design of Scott (1952:113), was set on alternate days in the settlement and the forest. No flies were caught during the four days the trap was set in the forest but a total of six flies were caught in the eight days that the trap was set in the settlement. Housefly density in the settlement is still extremely low compared to more heavily populated agricultural regions such as China where an average of 16 flies per trapping hour were caught in a series of experiments reported in Scott (1952:109-10).

Bees and wasps also appear to adapt well to living in the settlement. A large colony of wasps was established in the framework of an abandoned house.

Introduction of New Species

The Semang at Sungai Rual keep a few domestic animals, principally dogs, cats, and fowl. None are numerous: there are five or six dogs, four or five chickens, two cats, and a solitary muscovy duck. All except the dogs were purchased from the Malays and are kept as pets for varying lengths of time. Two of the bands keep dogs but they are out of favor with the other groups as it is believed that they attract elephants to the settlement. None of the domesticated animals are able to survive on their own in the forest and their numbers are so few that they can have little impact on the forest ecosystem, although presence of the dogs may tend to scare wild mammals away from the vicinity of the settlement.

5
Conclusions
The Evolution of Human Relations with the Environment

This monograph bears the deliberately provocative title of "Primitive Polluters." It was selected in order to bring into dramatic juxtaposition concepts that in modern Western thought are generally treated as being diametrically opposite. Primitive is commonly linked with pristine and beautiful, civilized with degraded and ugly. Despite some ambiguity stemming from the residual influence of the Hobbesian notion of primitive life being as vicious and brutal as it is short, it is the Rousseauian view that has largely prevailed. The noble savage, living in harmony with both his fellow creatures and Mother Nature, is a recurrent figure not only in popular literature but in anthropological monographs as well. Margaret Mead's ethnographic portrayal of Samoans as the gentle inhabitants of an idyllic tropical paradise offers perhaps the best known example of this romantic vision of primitive human ecology. Colin Turnbull's portrayal of the Mbuti Pygmies is a more recent example of this genre. From this perspective, it is the evolution of civilized society that is made to bear the blame not only for man's inhumanity to man but also for the despoilation of the environment. Even many Marxists, despite their avowed materialism, look back with nostalgia to the halcyon days of primitive communism when they imagine that there were no contradictions among humans or between humans and nature.

The drawing of a fundamental distinction between primitive and civilized is actually an anti-evolutionary position, although it is generally mistaken for an evolutionary point of view. By assimilating primitive people to the natural world—in effect viewing them as more animal-like than civilized people—this perspective obscures the fact that all humans, regardless of the stage they occupy on the social evolutionary continuum, are distinguished from all other species by their participation in what Leslie White (1975) refers to as cultural systems, and what are called social systems in this work. It is because of the activities they perform to keep these systems functioning, and not simply the meeting of their individual biological needs, that the impact of people on nature is distinct from that of other species.

Although undoubtedly the transition from our animal past to our present culture-bearing status was long and gradual, and it is impossible to pinpoint exactly when the threshold was crossed, all existing human social systems clearly represent a distinct evolutionary level having unique emergent properties. They capture free energy from the environment and use it to manipulate materials and information for purposes of system self-organization and survival. Their functioning necessarily affects the flow of energy, materials and information in the ecosystems with which they interact, causing the structure and functioning of these ecosystems to change in response. Larger, more powerful social systems might be expected to exert more intensive and wider ranging ecological impacts than smaller, less powerful ones, but these differences are quantitative rather than qualitative. The evolution of human relations with the environment constitutes a single, unbroken continuum rather than any absolute dichotomy between primitive and civilized societies. If there is a dichotomy involved here, it is between the human species and all others, i.e., between the one species with culture and all those species without it.

On the whole, I think that the evidence presented in chapter 4 demonstrates the essential functional similarity of the environmental interactions of primitive and civilized societies. The Semang are involved in exchanges of energy, materials, and information with their ecosystem no different in kind from those carried out by modern industrial societies. These flows produce comparable types of environmental impacts. Pollution of the air by domestic fires or burning of swidden fields, pollution of water by introduction of disease organisms or fish poison, pollution of soil by indiscriminate dumping of rubbish, are all environmental impacts which are qualitatively no different than those so loudly deplored when they result from the activities of civilized societies.

What is more surprising than the fact that Semang produce measurable impacts on their environment, is the evidence suggesting that these impacts, at least at the local scale, are not invariably quantitatively less significant than ours, despite the immense differences in technological power between primitive and modern societies. This was not something that I had expected to find when I began this research. I too accepted a gradualistic view of the evolution of human impacts on the environment. It seemed logical to assume that the impacts of primitive peoples, although real and measurable, would be of lower magnitude than those of larger and more powerful social systems. But first-hand observations directly challenged this view and forced modification of my position, as the following extract from my field notes reveals:

> The smoke in Mat Dinh's house was quite thick—like at a winter-time Washington cocktail party after about three hours. The *atap* [thatching] is glossy black over most of the roof. It looks to me now that man initially pollutes his immediate external environment (house interior, settlement site) and his internal environment (e.g., his lungs via smoking) and only later begins to significantly impact the larger environment.

The Semang showed me that even primitive people can have a major impact on their environment at the local level. Although the Semang do not cause significant air pollution at the regional or global level, they achieve quite respectable pollution levels in terms of the immediate life space of the individual and the household. Burning of domestic fires and heavy smoking of cigarettes results in atmospheric contamination with noxious gases and particulate matter equalling or surpassing the norm in modern industrial cities. If citizens of Malaysia's capital city of Kuala Lumpur were confronted with air pollution of the intensity normal in Semang households they would rise up in outrage over the terrible state of the city's environment, and they would blame it on modernization and capitalist industrialization.

Of course the geographical scale at which human impacts are evident does appear to change in the course of cultural evolution. Because of their small numbers, limited sources of energy, and low-powered technology, the Semang are simply unable to exert extensive influence on the Malaysian tropical rain forest ecosystem as a whole. Their activities can pollute the few cubic meters of atmosphere within a shelter or change the microclimate of a swidden field covering a few hectares. The extent of the forest is so great and the size and power of the Semang social system so limited, however, that its total ecological impact offers only a faint indication of the environmental change that can occur when the full force of an industrialized social system is brought to bear on nature.

Nevertheless, primitive peoples do cause significant environmental change. Such transformation is an inevitable concomitant of the evolution of culture as a superorganic phenomenon rather than an aberration reflecting some unique moral flaw in modern civilized societies. The environment is changed away from its natural state, not because of human greed or maliciousness, but simply because continued existence of all social systems necessitates it. Primitive or civilized alike, we are all polluters because we are all members of social systems, the survival of which is contingent on continuous modification of the natural world.

The environmental problems of modern society cannot, therefore, be solved by individual moral reformation, by returning to the supposed "ecological wisdom" of the primitive cultures. Certainly values and attitudes can influence our behavior and thus more responsible attitudes regarding human relations with the environment can help to ameliorate our worst excesses. But the real heart of the problem lies in the evolution of vast and powerful social systems incorporating billions of people and bringing virtually the entire biosphere within their fields of influence. It is only by understanding the behavior of these systems as systems, and using this understanding to try to modify the way they function, that we can hope, however faintly, to influence the future evolution of human relations with the environment.

Plates

Plate 1. A Semang band returns to the settlement from a collecting trip in the forest.

84

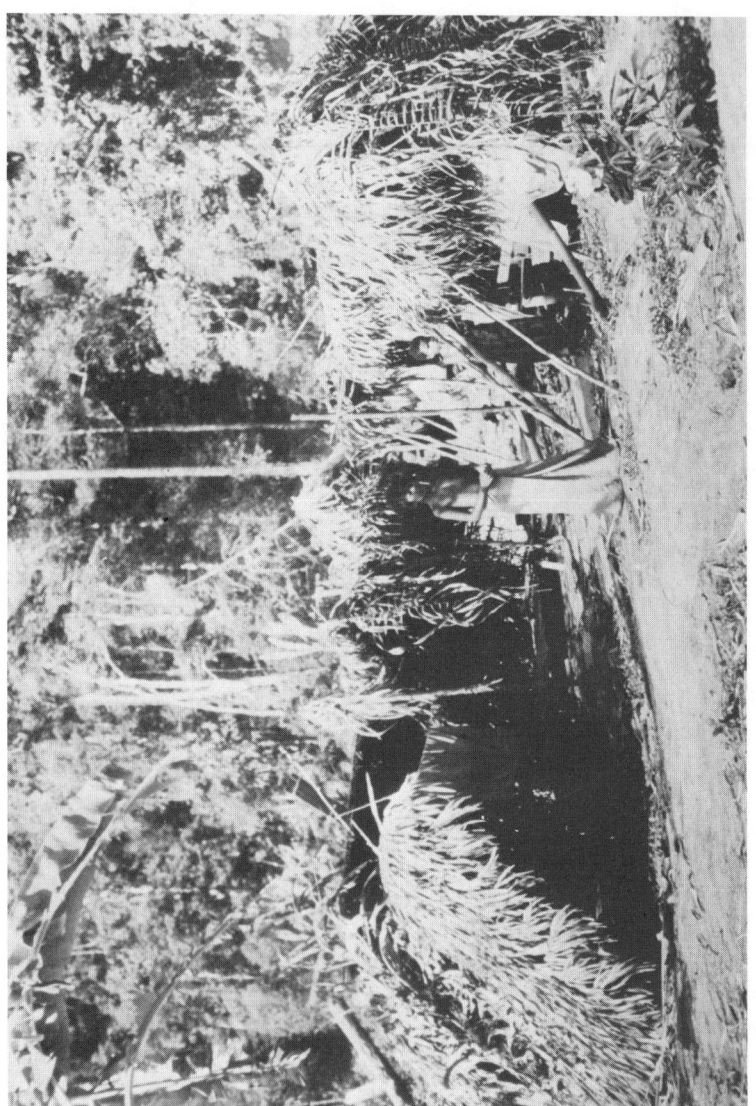

Plate 2. Traditional-style lean-tos.

Plate 3. A Semang family inside their lean-to.

Plate 4. The resettlement at Sungai Rual. The houses are surrounded by the swidden field. Primary forest is in the background.

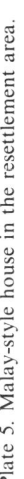

Plate 5. Malay-style house in the resettlement area.

Plate 6. Living area underneath a house in the resettlement. Note the trash discarded on the ground.

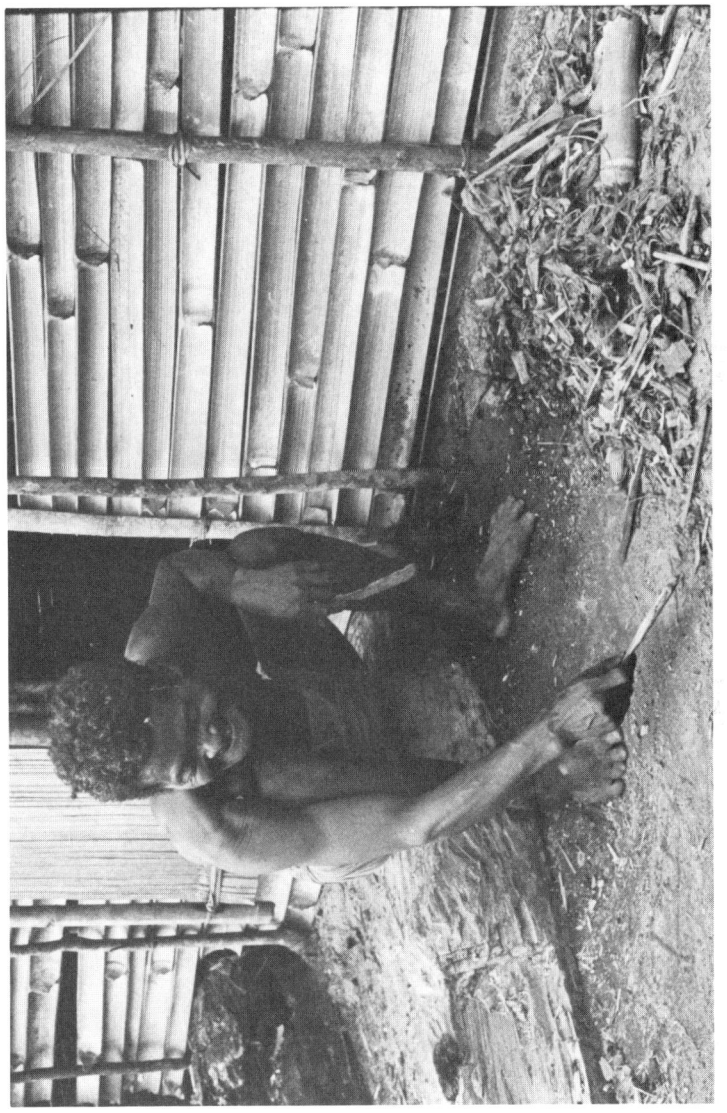

Plate 7. Semang man clearing rubbish away from his front door.

Plate 8. Semang man heating blowpipe darts over smokey fire inside house.

Plate 9. Felling a tree in the primary forest to clear a swidden.

Plate 10. Semang woman clearing undergrowth to make a new swidden.

Plate 11. Semang woman carrying home firewood from the forest.

Plate 12. Semang hunters bringing wild pig meat home from the forest.

Plate 13. Semang woman shelling *petai* seeds collected from the forest. Later they will be sold to merchants in Kampung Jeli.

Plate 14. Semang boy holding captive wild birds that are being raised as pets.

Plate 15. Smoke from the domestic hearth drifting through the roof of a house in the resettlement.

Plate 16. A young Semang drinking tea in a shop in Kampung Jeli. Photo by Alberto Gomes.

References

Abdul Rashid B. Idris
    1976   *The Jahai Negritos at Sungei Rual Resettlement, Kelantan: A Brief Study on the Social Organisation of a Tribal Community in Malaysia*. Unpublished graduation exercise, Kuala Lumpur, University of Malaya, Department of Anthropology and Sociology.

Alias Mohd. Ali
    1976   *Aktiviti "Memburu-Menghimpun" (Hunting-Gathering) Di Kalangan Orang Jahai Negrito Di Kawasan Penempatan Semula Orang-Orang Asli di Pos Sungei Rual, Tanah Merah, Kelantan*. Unpublished graduation exercise, Kuala Lumpur, University of Malaya, Department of Anthropology and Sociology.

Anderson, Edgar
    1967   *Plants, Man and Life*. Berkeley: University of California Press.

Bates, Marston
    1956   Man as an agent in the spread of organisms. In W. L. Thomas (ed.), *Man's Role in Changing the Face of the Earth*, pp. 788–804. Chicago: University of Chicago Press.

Benjamin, Geoffrey
    1973   Introduction. In P. Schebesta, *Among the Forest Dwarfs of Malaya*, pp. v–xiv. Kuala Lumpur: Oxford University Press.

Bennett, John W.
    1976   *The Ecological Transition: Cultural Anthropology and Human Adaptation*. New York: Pergamon Press.

Bodley, John H.
    1976   *Anthropology and Contemporary Human Problems*. Menlo Park, Calif.: Cummings Publishing Company.

Carey, Iskandar
    1976   *The Orang Asli: The Aboriginal Tribes of Peninsular Malaysia*. Kuala Lumpur: Oxford University Press.

Castagnol, E. M.
    1939   Methode d'analyse du sol appliquée à la recherche des emplacements anciennement habits. *Institut Indochinois pour l'Etude de l'Homme, Bulletins et Travaux* 2:191–201.

Chang, T. T.
    1984   Conservation of rice genetic resources: Luxury or necessity? *Science* 224:251–256.

Committee on Effects of Herbicides in Vietnam
    1974   *The Effects of Herbicides in South Vietnam.* Washington D.C.: National Academy of Sciences.
Conway, Gordon R.
    1972   Ecological aspects of pest control in Malaysia. In M. T. Farvar and J. P. Milton (eds.), *The Careless Technology,* pp. 467–488. Garden City: Natural History Press.
Conway, Gordon R. and David S. McCauley
    1983   Intensifying tropical agriculture: The Indonesian experience. *Nature* 302(5906):288–289.
Cook, Earl
    1971   The flow of energy in an industrial society. *Scientific American* 224(3):135–144.
Cooper, John M.
    1940   Andamanese-Semang-Eta cultural relations. *Primitive Man* 13:29–47.
Cumberland, Kenneth B.
    1963   Man's role in modifying island environments in the Southwest Pacific: with special reference to New Zealand. In F. R. Fosberg (ed.), *Man's Role in the Island Ecosystem,* pp. 186–206. Honolulu: Bishop Museum Press.
Dale, Tom and Vernon G. Carter
    1955   *Topsoil and Civilization.* Norman: University of Oklahoma Press.
Dunn, Frederick L.
    1972   Intestinal parasitism in Malayan aborigines (Orang Asli). *World Health Organization Bulletin* 46(1):99–114.
    1975   *Rain-forest Collectors and Traders: A Study of Resource Utilization in Modern and Ancient Malaya.* Kuala Lumpur: Monographs of the Malaysian Branch, Royal Asiatic Society No. 5.
Eckholm, Erik
    1978   *Disappearing Species: The Social Challenge.* Worldwatch Paper 22, Washington D.C.: Worldwatch Institute.
Eckholm, Erik and Lester R. Brown
    1977   *Spreading Deserts—The Hand of Man.* Worldwatch Paper 13, Washington D.C.: Worldwatch Institute.
Ehrlich, P. R. et al.
    1984   Long-term biological consequences of nuclear war. *Science* 222:1293–1300.
Elton, Charles S.
    1958   *The Ecology of Invasions by Animals and Plants.* London: Methuen.
Endicott, Kirk
    1979   *Batek Negrito Religion.* Oxford: Clarendon Press.
Evans, Igor H. N.
    1937   *The Negritos of Malaya.* Cambridge: University Press.
Farvar, M. Taghi and John Milton
    1972   *The Careless Technology.* Garden City: Natural History Press.
Fosberg, F. R. (ed.)
    1963   *Man's Place in the Island Ecosystem.* Honolulu: Bishop Museum Press.
Fox, Richard G.
    1969   "Professional primitives": Hunters and gatherers of nuclear South Asia. *Man in India* 49(2):139–160.
Gomes, Alberto G.
    1976   *A Social Demography of Jahai Negritos at Rual Post, Kelantan.* Unpublished graduation exercise, Kuala Lumpur, University of Malaya, Department of Anthropology and Sociology.
    1979   *Ecological Adaptation and Population Change: A Comparative Study of Semang Foragers and Temuan Horticulturalists.* Unpublished M.A. thesis, Kuala Lumpur, University of Malaya, Department of Anthropology and Sociology.

1982 *Ecological Adaptation and Population Change: Semang Foragers and Temuan Horticulturalists in West Malaysia.* East-West Environment and Policy Institute Research Report, No. 12. Honolulu: East-West Center.

Gorman, Chester
    1971   The Hoabinhian and after: Subsistence patterns in Southeast Asia during the Late Pleistocene and Early Recent periods. *World Archaeology* 2(3):300–320.

Guthrie, D. A.
    1971   Primitive man's relation to nature. *BioScience* 21:721–723.

Harp, Elmer Jr.
    1974   Threshold indicators of culture in air photo archaeology: A case study in the arctic. In E. Vogt (ed.), *Aerial Photography in Anthropological Field Research*, pp. 14–27. Cambridge, Mass.: Harvard University Press.

Harrisson, Tom and Barbara Harrisson
    1969-70   The prehistory of Sabah. *Sabah Society Journal* 4.

Heizer, Robert F.
    1955   Primitive man as an ecologic factor. *Kroeber Anthropological Society Papers*, No. 13:1–31.

Huntington, Ellsworth
    1959   *Mainsprings of Civilization.* New York: Mentor.

Hutterer, Karl L.
    1976   An evolutionary approach to the Southeast Asian cultural sequence. *Current Anthropology* 17(2):221–242.
    1977   Reinterpreting the Southeast Asian Paleolithic. In J. Allen, J. Golson and R. Jones (eds.), *Sunda and Sahul*, pp. 31–71. London: Academic Press.
    1983   The natural and cultural history of Southeast Asian agriculture: Ecological and evolutionary considerations. *Anthropos* 78(1/2):169–212.

Jacobson, Thorkild and Robert N. Adams
    1958   Salt and silt in ancient Mesopotamian agriculture. *Science* 128:1251–1258.

Jones, Rhys
    1969   Fire-stick farming. *Australian National History* 16:224–228.

Leigh, C.H. and K.S. Low
    1973   An appraisal of the flood situation in West Malaysia. In E. Soepadmo and K.G. Singh (eds.), *Proceedings of the Symposium on Biological Resources and National Development*, pp. 57–70. Kuala Lumpur: Malayan Nature Society.

Lewis, Henry T.
    1972   The role of fire in the domestication of plants and animals in Southwest Asia: a hypothesis. *Man* 7(2):195–222.
    1973   *Patterns of Indian Burning in California: Ecology and Ethnohistory.* Anthropological Papers 1. Ramona, Calif.: Ballena Press.

Lie-Injo, L. E., A. Fix, J. M. Bolton, and R. H. Gilman
    1972   Haemoglobin E-hereditary elliptoeytosis in Malayan Aborigines. *Acta Haematologica* 47:210–216.

Lowry, N. P.
    1967   The climate of cities. *Scientific American* 217(2):15–23.

McNeill, William H.
    1979   *Plagues and Peoples.* Garden City: Anchor Press/Doubleday.

Martin, Paul S. and H. E. Wright (eds.)
    1967   *Pleistocene Extinctions: The Search for a Cause.* New Haven: Yale University Press.

Medway, Lord
    1977   The Niah excavations and an assessment of the impact of early man on mammals in Borneo. *Asian Perspectives* 20:51–69.

Mellanby, Kenneth
    1972   *The Biology of Pollution.* The Institute of Biology's Studies in Biology, No. 38. London: Edward Arnold.
Murdock, George Peter
    1934   *Our Primitive Contemporaries.* New York: Macmillan.
National Research Council Committee on Genetic Vulnerability of Major Crops
    1972   *Genetic Vulnerability of Major Crops.* Washington, D.C.: National Academy of Sciences.
Nicholson, Max
    1971   Man's use of the earth: Historical background. In T. R. Detwyler (ed.), *Man's Impact on Environment,* pp. 10–21. New York: McGraw-Hill.
Noone, R. O. D.
    1955   Notes on the trade in blowpipes and blowpipe bamboo in North Malaya. *Federation Museums Journal* 1/2:1–18.
Olson, Storris L. and Helen F. James
    1982   Fossil birds from the Hawaiian Islands: Evidence for wholesale extinction by man before Western contact. *Science* 217:633–635.
Orlove, B. J.
    1980   Ecological anthropology. *Annual Review of Anthropology* 9:234–273.
Rambo, A. Terry
    1978   Bows, blowpipes and blunderbusses: Ecological implications of weapons change among the Malaysian Negritos. *Malayan Nature Journal* 32(2):209–216.
    1979a   A note on stone tool use by the Orang Asli (aborigines) of Peninsular Malaysia. *Asian Perspectives* 22(2):113–119.
    1979b   Primitive man's impact on genetic resources of the Malaysian tropical rain forest. *Malaysian Applied Biology* 8(1):59–65.
    1980a   Fire and the energy efficiency of swidden agriculture. *Asian Perspectives* 23(2):309–316.
    1980b   Of stones and stars: Malaysian Orang Asli environmental knowledge in relation to their adaptation to the tropical rain forest ecosystem. *Federation Museums Journal* 25 N.S.:77–88.
    1982a   Human ecology research on tropical agroecosystems in Southeast Asia. *Singapore Journal of Tropical Geography* 3(1):86–99.
    1982b   Orang Asli adaptive strategies: Implications for Malaysian natural resource development planning. In C. MacAndrews and L. S. Chia (eds.), *Too Rapid Rural Development,* pp. 251–299. Athens, Ohio: Ohio University Press.
    1983   *Conceptual Approaches to Human Ecology.* East-West Environment and Policy Institute Research Report, No. 14. Honolulu: East-West Center.
Reich, Charles A.
    1970   *The Greening of America.* New York: Random House.
Ridley, H. N.
    1930   *The Dispersal of Plants Throughout the World.* Ashford, Kent: L. Reeve and Co.
Root, Barry F.
    1976   An estimate of annual global atmospheric pollutant emissions from grassland fires and agricultural burning in the tropics. *Professional Geographer* 28(4):349–352.
Schebesta, Paul
    1952   *Die Negrito Asiens,* Vol. I. Wien-Modling: St.-Gabriel-Verlag.
    1954   *Die Negrito Asiens,* Vol. II. Wien-Modling: St.-Gabriel-Verlag. [English translation by Human Relations Area Files.]
    1957   *Die Negrito Asiens,* Vol. III. Wien-Modling: St.-Gabriel-Verlag. [English translation by Human Relations Area Files.]
    1973   *Among the Forest Dwarfs of Malaya.* Kuala Lumpur: Oxford University Press.

References

Scott, J. C.
    1952   *Health and Agriculture in China.* London: Faber and Faber.

Service, Elman R.
    1962   *Primitive Social Organization: An Evolutionary Perspective.* New York: Random House.

Sham Sani
    1979   *Aspects of Air Pollution Climatology in a Tropical City: A Case of Kuala Lumpur-Petaling Jaya Malaysia.* Bangi: Universiti Kebangsaan Malaysia Press.

Simmons, I. G.
    1974   *The Ecology of Natural Resources.* London: Edward Arnold.

Smith, Kirk R., A. L. Aggarwal, and M. R. Dave
    1983   Air pollution and rural biomass fuels in developing countries. *Atmospheric Environment* 17(11):2343–2362.

Smith, Philip E. L.
    1972   *The Consequences of Food Production.* Addison-Wesley Module in Anthropology, 31. Reading, Mass.: Addison-Wesley.

Solheim, Wilhelm G. II
    1972   Early man in Southeast Asia, pp. 25–31. *Expedition*, 14(3):25–31.

Southwick, Charles H.
    1976   *Ecology and the Quality of Our Environment.* New York: Van Nostrand.

Steward, Julian H.
    1955   *Theory and Method of Culture Change: The Methodology of Multilinear Evolution.* Urbana: University of Illinois Press.

Steward, Omar C.
    1956   Fire as the first great force employed by man. In W. L. Thomas (ed.), *Man's Role in Changing the Face of the Earth*, pp. 115–133. Chicago: University of Chicago Press.

Taylor, Rubert
    1975   *Noise*, 2nd edition. Middlesex: Penguin Books.

Tuan, Yi-fu
    1968   Discrepancies between environmental attitude and behaviour: Examples from Europe and China. *Canadian Geographer* 12(3):176–191.

Vayda, Andrew P. and Roy A. Rappaport
    1968   Ecology: Cultural and non-cultural. In J. A. Clifton (ed.), *Introduction to Cultural Anthropology*, pp. 476–497. Boston: Houghton-Mifflin Co.

Walker, Anthony R.
    1976   The swidden economy of a Lahu Nyi (Red Lahu) village community in North Thailand. *Folk* 18:145–188.

Wallerstein, Immanuel
    1980   *The Modern World-System: Capitalist Agriculture and the Origins of the European World-Economy in the Sixteenth Century.* New York: Academic Press.

Westing, Arthur H.
    1984   The remnants of war. *Ambio* 13(1):14–17.

White, Leslie A.
    1943   Energy and the evolution of culture. *American Anthropologist* 45:335–356.
    1975   *The Concept of Cultural Systems: A Key to Understanding Tribes and Nations.* New York: Columbia University Press.

White, Lynn
    1967   The historical roots of our ecologic crisis. *Science* 155:1203–1207.

Wolf, Eric R.
    1982   *Europe and the People without History.* Berkeley: University of California Press.

Woodwell, George M., Paul P. Craig, and Norton A. Johnson
    1971   DDT in the biosphere: Where does it go? *Science* 174: 1101–1107.
Woodwell, George M., Charles F. Wurster, Jr. and Peter A. Isaacson
    1967   DDT residues in and East Coast estuary: A case of biological concentration of a persistent insecticide. *Science* 156:821–824.
Yong Hoi Sen
    1979   Genetic resources of terrestrial animals in Malaysia. *Malaysian Applied Biology* 8(1):67–72.

Scott, J. C.
    1952   *Health and Agriculture in China.* London: Faber and Faber.
Service, Elman R.
    1962   *Primitive Social Organization: An Evolutionary Perspective.* New York: Random House.
Sham Sani
    1979   *Aspects of Air Pollution Climatology in a Tropical City: A Case of Kuala Lumpur-Petaling Jaya Malaysia.* Bangi: Universiti Kebangsaan Malaysia Press.
Simmons, I. G.
    1974   *The Ecology of Natural Resources.* London: Edward Arnold.
Smith, Kirk R., A. L. Aggarwal, and M. R. Dave
    1983   Air pollution and rural biomass fuels in developing countries. *Atmospheric Environment* 17(11):2343-2362.
Smith, Philip E. L.
    1972   *The Consequences of Food Production.* Addison-Wesley Module in Anthropology, 31. Reading, Mass.: Addison-Wesley.
Solheim, Wilhelm G. II
    1972   Early man in Southeast Asia, pp. 25-31. *Expedition,* 14(3):25-31.
Southwick, Charles H.
    1976   *Ecology and the Quality of Our Environment.* New York: Van Nostrand.
Steward, Julian H.
    1955   *Theory and Method of Culture Change: The Methodology of Multilinear Evolution.* Urbana: University of Illinois Press.
Steward, Omar C.
    1956   Fire as the first great force employed by man. In W. L. Thomas (ed.), *Man's Role in Changing the Face of the Earth,* pp. 115-133. Chicago: University of Chicago Press.
Taylor, Rubert
    1975   *Noise,* 2nd edition. Middlesex: Penguin Books.
Tuan, Yi-fu
    1968   Discrepancies between environmental attitude and behaviour: Examples from Europe and China. *Canadian Geographer* 12(3):176-191.
Vayda, Andrew P. and Roy A. Rappaport
    1968   Ecology: Cultural and non-cultural. In J. A. Clifton (ed.), *Introduction to Cultural Anthropology,* pp. 476-497. Boston: Houghton-Mifflin Co.
Walker, Anthony R.
    1976   The swidden economy of a Lahu Nyi (Red Lahu) village community in North Thailand. *Folk* 18:145-188.
Wallerstein, Immanuel
    1980   *The Modern World-System: Capitalist Agriculture and the Origins of the European World-Economy in the Sixteenth Century.* New York: Academic Press.
Westing, Arthur H.
    1984   The remnants of war. *Ambio* 13(1):14-17.
White, Leslie A.
    1943   Energy and the evolution of culture. *American Anthropologist* 45:335-356.
    1975   *The Concept of Cultural Systems: A Key to Understanding Tribes and Nations.* New York: Columbia University Press.
White, Lynn
    1967   The historical roots of our ecologic crisis. *Science* 155:1203-1207.
Wolf, Eric R.
    1982   *Europe and the People without History.* Berkeley: University of California Press.

Woodwell, George M., Paul P. Craig, and Norton A. Johnson
   1971   DDT in the biosphere: Where does it go? *Science* 174: 1101–1107.
Woodwell, George M., Charles F. Wurster, Jr. and Peter A. Isaacson
   1967   DDT residues in and East Coast estuary: A case of biological concentration of a persistent insecticide. *Science* 156:821–824.
Yong Hoi Sen
   1979   Genetic resources of terrestrial animals in Malaysia. *Malaysian Applied Biology* 8(1):67–72.